Mag

YOU

Barbra White

For further copies of: **Magnificent *YOU***
"Accept The Innate Greatness You Are ... And You Will Heal The World By Your Living Example."

Order online: www.acceptedasiam.com

Magnificent *YOU*
"Accept The Innate Greatness You Are ... And You Will Heal The World By Your Living Example."

Cover Design by Tara
Copyright © 2010
by Barbra White

All Rights Reserved
No part of this book may be reproduced without written consent from the publisher.

ISBN: 978-0-9830623-0-1

Accepted As I Am Retreat Center
157 S. Mill
Plymouth, Michigan 48170
734-455-1438

Acknowledgements

I know that when we follow our hearts, Life provides. I have taken many leaps in following my dreams and heart. God-Life always supported me. My Life is the life of God. Thank you.

Where God guides, God will provide. Even when I thought I wasn't being supported, as I consciously went through the pain and kept my heart open; Life/God seduced me into my next level of greatness.

Thank you to every person who gave me the honor of guiding them. I learned from every session and every word I was guided to say. Many times, I would rush to write down what I said in session because it was exactly what I needed to hear or it correlated with a workshop I was working on.

Thank you to my family for believing in me. That is the greatest gift you all have given me. Thank you Suzanne, Robert, Linnea, Danielle, Scott, and Barbara.

Thank you to my previous romantic relationships. It taught me what love was not, so that I could know what love truly is and where love truly is. Years of trying to make love happen in others showed me clearly the Love always was within. Thank you for the Love I now have in my life.

Thank you to the amazing spiritual mentors I have had, Dr. Shear, Pittaway, Dad, Monk Mahdi, Penny, Shinto, Marilyn, and many more.

Thank you to Jennifer, Kay, Erin, Kim, and Davis for helping me to surrender to the universal process of healing and take ownership over my life.

Thank you Suzanne (mom) for hours and hours of editing and support.

Thank you to every aspect of God, supporting me, from my dogs, to the sunshine, to all the synchronicities that guided me in the right direction. Thank you for my willingness to see it.

Thank you for my willingness to open to friends, support, and love. With that said, thank you to: Joe, Deanna, Mary L, Angela, Josh, Jill, Mary B, Tara, Dory, Amy, Tina, Katrina, Leo, Chelle, Kathleen, Colleen, Valarie, and Janet. Thank you to Sheryl and Lynn for inspiring me to put this book together. Thank you. Thank you to Al and Sandi of Insights for inspiring people to express their talents. Thank you Matt, Amy, and Tina from Radish Creative Group for developing the CDs. Thank you to Penny and Howard of Body Mind Spirit Guide. Penny you were instrumental to providing the vehicle to God's teachings, expressing through me.

Thank you Life, thank you Joy, thank you for all the good I've already been created to be. Thank you for an avenue to express the wisdom God has given me. Thank you for this inner wisdom and ability to inspire others into their innate greatness. Thank you for the Love that Just Is and that every time I breathe, I can feel God in me, as me and around me. Thank you.

Dedication

I dedicate this book to the methods and organizations that helped me to stay awake to the reality of Love and God.

Agape International Spiritual Center—Dr Michael Bernard Beckwith

Sedona Method

Bikram Yoga

Pramahansa Yogananda and the Self-Realization Fellowship

I intend to attract all those who will benefit from my enlightenment process, as well as, I benefit from there process. With that said, I dedicate this book to all my clients; who have helped me more than they know. Through the process of helping people to wake up to their God given innate magnificence, I came to know my own on a greater level. Thank you.

Table of Contents

Introduction		9
Chapter 1:	Remembering Your Magnificence!!!	13
Chapter 2:	Love Will Set You Free!!!!	21
Chapter 3:	Happiness = Realizing Yourself as Love-God	29
Chapter 4:	"Shame Blame Game"	39
Chapter 5:	Taking Full Responsibility for Your Own Life	51
Chapter 6:	Love is Who We Are	59
Chapter 7:	Transforming from Ego to Essence	67
Chapter 8:	One light, One power, One presence	77
Chapter 9:	What is power, and how do I get it????	87
Chapter 10:	Why Are We All So Lonely?	95
Chapter 11:	Sing Your Greatness into the World!!!	101
Chapter 12:	Your Life is an Expression of God	109
Chapter 13:	Engaging Your Spiritual Warrior Within	123
Chapter 14:	Delicious Abundance Is Waiting	131
Chapter 15:	Accept the Love You Are! You Are Already Worthy and Uniquely Gifted!	139
Chapter 16:	Simply Be Open and All Your Desires Will Happen	145
Chapter 17:	What Is Love??????	153
Chapter 18:	What Kind of "Bug" Are You???	161

Chapter 19:	How to Heal the World in Three Easy Steps!	167
Chapter 20:	Stand In Your Power as Love	175
Chapter 21:	Tao of Dog	183
Chapter 22:	Living In Integrity with Self	193
Chapter 23:	You Have a Choice	201
Chapter 24:	Let Your Voice Be Heard!!!!!!	209
Chapter 25:	You are Beautiful Now	227
Chapter 26:	Encouragement	237
	Affirmation	243
	About the Author	245

Introduction

You are magnificent!!

What if you were to accept that **fully** right now? How would your life change? How would your choices change? Would you continue to put up with the things you do now? What dreams would you begin to believe in again?

This little book's intent is to begin to get you to think of yourself differently. How you perceive yourself is how you will perceive the world. We let our unexamined perceptions run our lives. Isn't it time to look at what you truly believe about yourself and see if it is empowering you?

These writings come from my 20,000 hours of self-acceptance healing sessions with clients of various backgrounds, ethnicities and problems. It also comes from self-acceptance workshops and retreats I have led, and from personal life lessons. I have seen the wisdom offered in these pages empower people and change lives.

If something resonates with you in these pages, then use it. If something strikes an emotional chord, then take a moment to look within. But, if something doesn't resonate with you or strike a cord, then simply let it go. Always follow your heart or gut. You are your own best guide.

Every person or thing is a reflection of what you feel about yourself. You cannot see in another what you haven't seen in yourself. See your own greatness, and then you can see it in another. Believe your faults are the truth of who you are, and then you will tend to focus on that in another. Learn to love and thus release your perceived faults, and you will free your soul. Free your soul and you will free another by your living example.

Love yourself, and you will be the change you wish to see in the world. Self-realization or self-love will change your life. Your life is a reflection of what you believe about yourself.

Your Soul, Authentic Self, Essence or True Identity is that of magnificence, beauty, and Love. We mistake ourselves to be our humanness; the mind, body, and emotions. We forget that the mind, body, and emotions are just a small part of who we are. To know yourself as your already present magnificence, you must love your humanness—this is the paradox. This is why loving yourself will naturally uncover the greatness you already have been created to be.

Each chapter stands alone in its ability to guide you into a greater awareness of universal truths of Love-God-and Self Acceptance. Feel free to jump around in the book and read a chapter that speaks to you in the moment. You can, however, read the book in a linear fashion if that is what you enjoy.

As you read, if you take the time to ponder a statement that "strikes a chord" with you, then this book has the potential to change your life. The intent of this material is that you come to know a greater more magnificent version of yourself.

1

Remembering Your Magnificence!!!

Remembering Your Magnificence!!!

Why don't we know how amazing we really are? If we are each a complete piece of God, why don't we feel this all the time? This temporary amnesia of our own greatness is because we have all been taught a distorted form of "love." Remembering the magnificence of who you truly are is a process of reprogramming your mind to what love really is. Our innate human desire is to feel loved and to give love. At our core, we all just want to feel loved, but bless our hearts, we really don't know what love is.

We desperately look for love in things, people, and conditions being met. We struggle and suffer as we try to hold unto this "love," painfully losing it and fighting for it. Until one day, we decide there has to be a better way, and that life really should be easier and full of joy: we surrender, give up the fight, and we courageously let go. At this point, we are not sure of what this letting go will bring, but the pain of trying to control this "love" has reached its maximum pain threshold.

We believe that this thing we are letting go of ... IS LOVE. The goal, the money, the opinion of our peers, and the happiness of our children is what we have based our happiness on. You ask, "How can I be happy when my world is falling apart?" My reply to you would be, "How does your worrying about it and fighting it help?"

Feeling good is feeling God; or another way to say this is, feeling good is feeling lovable. Something only has the power to "make us feel bad" when we have unknowingly attached our worthiness to it. Someone only has the power to "make us feel bad" when we have unconsciously attached our worthiness to their opinions and actions.

The process of realizing our innate gifts, and our inner potential, is a process of letting go. It is only when we have let go of the thing that we think '"will cause us to die" if we don't have, do we realize the life inside of each of us. In other words, it is only when we let go of the rotten apple do we realize the banquet within.

This thing we think will make us lovable is outside of us. When we have it, we feel good-God, and when we don't, we feel bad. It is like an addiction: doing, giving, working, proving, pleasing, controlling, fixing to find our sense of self. *In the journey of living a conscious life, we all are learning what true unconditional love is, by recognizing what love is not.* We discover our magnificence within us by admitting and *forgiving* how we are attached to outside validation.

Letting go can be very scary because we don't know what is on the other side. In truth, what we are really scared of is our own light because, *what is on the other side is our greatness, our gifts, and our greatest potential.* Our mind believes that if we let go of needing money or approval, then we will never have it. Our minds convince us if we let go of worrying about the future or our children, then something bad will happen. Our minds can't make sense of this, but the truth is, once we let go of this outside love, we will now have an abundance of the very thing we let go of. We realize the abundance within, and then we attract even more of that abundance.

We ask, "Why would God want me to let go of needing Love?" God doesn't want you to let go of needing love, just the love outside of yourself. Seek first the kingdom of heaven, and all else will be added unto you, <u>or love yourself first, and then love will be added unto you.</u> Be your own best friend, be on your own side, and love yourself, otherwise life will be a continual addictive chase to find feeling good, feeling God. Loving yourself means to know your complete and utter worthiness independent of outside conditions, opinions of others, or the outcome: to know the universe and to know God, focus on knowing yourself.

There are three main ingredients to letting go and discovering your inner magnificence.

1. A person needs a burning desire to know God-Spirit-Life-Love-Creation and/or SELF on a deeper level. This inner calling is the most important ingredient, but it must be paired with the following.

2. A willingness to look within: a willingness to stop blaming what you feel on outside things and people, and to feel your emotions with forgiveness, conscious awareness, and non-reaction.

3. A willingness to change your mind and see yourself and your world differently.

Have these three ingredients active and *your world will line up for your greatest good.* Everything in your life will begin to happen to show you and teach you about your lovability and preciousness. It's like the old saying, "Pray for patience, and you will be stuck in lines;" this works with self-acceptance and self-realization, as well. Pray to know the love and God within, and your life will now transform for that purpose. Trust the process; it is there for us all. The universe is yearning for your happiness, and God is seducing you to realize the magnificent truth of yourself.

Letting go, and/or self-acceptance is a continual process of changing our perception from love being outside of ourselves to love being within. This is a continual process of greater and sustainable inner joy, peace, and abundance.

2

Love Will Set You Free!!!!

Love Will Set You Free!!!!

Self-acceptance is based on the spiritual fact that LOVE is the foundation of who you are. You already are lovable. All that you desire already is here, waiting for you to let it in. Creation already has given fully of itself, AS ITSELF. You are like a ray of sun, a full representation of the sun, here to shine your light, and not just to battle *back,* to the sun. *You are here to show the world what self-love looks like, or in other words, to create heaven on Earth. You do this, by remembering who you are and living your life in the greatest joy.* Life is Love, or Life is God.

If you are trying too hard to "create" it, or to "make it" happen, you will sabotage yourself. In trying too hard and thinking the action is what *makes* things happen, we miss the point of life entirely. Our lives are supported and orchestrated by the divine within us and around us. It doesn't rest on our shoulders to get things done. *The action only is the next logical step to what we know to be true but not what actually makes it happen.*

There is nothing we need to do to "make" our lives happen; that already is "done." This is "done" by our past lives lived and the lives we are living today because we are eternal. We never die, and we are never born. There is NO "there" to reach, or obtain, for we already are "there." *The paradox is, believe you need to "get there," and you will never "get there."* <u>There is here</u>. Once this truth is realized within, true happiness is obtained.

We are all expanding in our awareness, of the reality of God, as who we are. This is the process of self-acceptance, or enlightenment, and it continues for the rest of your life. This is the adventure of a life lived *in,* and *as* Love-God. We will always be discovering another layer of truth, joy, wisdom, God, and Self. You are complete and incomplete in your awareness. As you become aware of another level of who you are, heaven is brought to Earth.

From this awareness, you and your life naturally expand to greater joy, peace, and abundance. The physical world has to respond to your changed awareness. *Change how you see yourself, and your world will change.* You are continually awakening to more of your Authentic Self and never less. As you continue to grow in your awareness of your innate greatness, another expansion of God happens. This awareness ripples into the hearts of all humanity, healing the world simply by remembering who you truly are. This is what it means to "be the change you wish to see in the world"—Mahatma Gandhi.

The truth does not set you free. Knowing that if you eat that bag of cookies, and they will make you fat, *does not* set you free of eating them. Knowing that you are scared to stand up for yourself at your job does not empower you to speak. **The truth does not set you free; love does.** Loving and accepting yourself right where you are sets you free. Forgiving your overeating and loving your body leads to not eating the cookies. Loving the fear, which means to feel it without self-judgment, also will empower you to stand up for what you believe in at your job.

We are here to experience life, as life presents itself to us. But, remember, well-being abounds, and God is *for* you, <u>not</u> against you. Everything *is* working out for your greatest good and highest joy. We have a choice to be on our own side or not. If we choose the path of self-love and self-acceptance, we learn our lesson, and the course of life changes and expands.

There is a saying, "If you have gotten used to a change, then you are already two steps behind." All That Is God desires our happiness, and if we let go and trust life, life will lead us into greater joy.

But, we try to understand something before we will let it go. We try to analyze the painful emotion or the bad situation, thinking that if we could just *understand* "why" it is here, then it would go away! This is the folly of our logic that traps us in suffering and keeps us, and our painful situations, from changing! Accept, forgive, and allow the emotion, the situation, and especially yourself, as it is, and then understanding will come. *Seek first to love, and then the "why" will reveal itself.*

Your worthiness is not based on conditions and circumstances. You are already worthy; this is God's gift to you. Your environment does not define you: You define you. Your true identity is that of Love, beauty, and infinite potential.

Love is enough. Love and forgive yourself, and you will set yourself free. *The truth does not set you free; love does.* Knowing more details of your situation or self-analyzation will NOT create the happiness and growth you are seeking.

Bring Love to yourself, your pain and situation, and then transformation will happen. As a person comes to know the power of Love to transform themselves and situations, they will realize that the ultimate <u>truth IS LOVE</u>. The truth does not set you free; love does. But, the real Truth is Love.

3

Happiness = Realizing yourself as Love-God

Happiness = Realizing yourself as Love-God

WE think to suffer is holy. To be in bliss is "unrealistic." Happiness is an elusive concept to many, yet when I say suffering, it is immediately understood. What is happiness? What is suffering? Is it that we have become so familiar with suffering that happiness has now become foreign to us? What is happiness? Is it a new a car? Is it the smile on your child's face? Is it about something within yourself of which you are proud? What is suffering? Is it not getting what you want? Feeling worthless? Pain?

Suffering is judging ourselves for the pain we are feeling; feeling bad and then being mad at ourselves for feeling bad. What did I do wrong? Why is this happening? How did I create this? Judging our emotional pain creates a story into how we are to blame for what is causing our discomfort. We then try to find our value outside of ourselves.

If suffering really is the blame placed on ourselves and not the actual event or thing causing us pain, then why do we blame ourselves? Why do we feel bad for feeling bad? **Life will have pain but the judgment of it makes it suffering.** Judgment of our feelings creates the feeling of separation from Spirit-Love-God.

Judgment and Ego mean the exact same thing. We create escape patterns to avoid our feelings. These escape patterns can never be fulfilled because they are based on trying to find Love-God outside of ourselves. In these escape patterns, we try to find our value in how much we do, give to others, our reputation, amount of money, control of others etc. ... **We begin to identify ourselves** as these patterns instead of the spirit and love we are. Life is a case of mistaken identity.

Think of yourself as Three Bodies: Physical, Mental, and Emotional. These bodies are just bodies, neutral things, like a tree or a rock, not good or bad. The Three Bodies will fluctuate according to what guidance we need to be receiving.

For example:

> Body: Our bodies are our spirits' last-ditch efforts to get us to change. Once we ignore the emotional guidance our spirits try to get our attention in our bodies.

> Emotion: Any negative emotion is just a sign you are not keeping up with yourself. You are not allowing your greatness or your spirit to shine.

Mind: A mind racing is always a signal we are trying to avoid a feeling. We escape to our minds because many of us are so afraid to feel an emotion and accept our God-Selves.

The Fourth Body is your spiritual body. It is only when you are balanced in the three bodies that your spirit truly can express itself into the world.

Life is a case of mistaken identity. You are not just your body, mind, or emotions; they are just a very small part of all that is YOU. You are human and God. <u>Whatever we don't love, we become</u>, this is why self-judgment has led us to not know ourselves as Love-God.

Judging yourself is like pressing pause on the DVD player to "suffering scene" of your life. "I know I need to let go of this, but I can't." "I know I am letting him get to me." "I know I need to forgive and love myself." It is <u>not about the knowing</u>; that is all in your head. You can't affirm, think, or speak yourself into forgiveness and acceptance. It has to be done in the heart.

We have to feel the emotion first, and acceptance will be the result. **Letting go and acceptance are the end products of truly feeling our emotions.** The 4 steps of processing self-acceptance and true happiness:

1. Recognize and own your feelings.

2. Feel them without judgment of the feelings of others or yourself.

3. Letting go happens from step two.

4. The "why" comes in. Most try to skip step 2 and go to 4, trying to find the "why" before they have allowed the healing to happen.

Encouragement is enough; focusing on the good is enough. You can't give chocolate and broccoli in the same bite. The broccoli will ruin the chocolate. Give the encouragement (chocolate) without the criticism (broccoli). **We still don't believe love is enough, especially with ourselves. We think that if we accept it, as it is, it will get worse.** We get trapped into thinking a focus of self-encouragement will make us lazy. We become trapped into trying to think ourselves into happiness. We become trapped into thinking if we just ignore the emotion or pain, it will go away. **We become trapped into thinking someone or something has to change, so we can be happy.**

Temporary happiness is being happy only when your family is happy, happiness when you achieve a goal, happiness when the weekend comes, happiness only when my body feels good, happiness only when I am not feeling this emotion. **True happiness is simply and powerfully knowing that you are worthy, lovable, and ALL right as you are.** True happiness is not based on any condition being met, or a person meeting your needs. When we can blame our bad feelings on something outside of ourselves, it gives some relief. But this also puts the power outside of us, meaning we can't heal it. **When all our outside conditions have been met, and we still feel bad, we are forced to finally look within.**

No one can make you happy or make you sad. It is all about you. It is always about you loving yourself: It is NEVER about them. **Happiness simply is loving all the parts of you. Your happiness always is about you**; thank God-Love for this because then the power to feel good is in our own hands.

4

"Shame Blame Game"

"Shame Blame Game"

If you put an apple pie in the oven, wouldn't you expect to take an apple pie out? Well, if you put in a snake in the oven wouldn't you expect to take out a snake? What you put in, you get out. Better said, **what you focus on, you get more of.** We criticize ourselves for the emotion we are feeling, the situation we are in and/or any mistakes we make, thinking it will make us better.

If we were to totally love ourselves, then we would have better health, internal peace, love, and joy. Somehow, as people, we really have missed this basic point. We think if we criticize ourselves enough or are hard on ourselves that we will try harder. If the first ingredient is condemnation, then this leads to a self that feels unloved, unpeaceful, and over time gets very worn out.

My intent is to convince you that loving yourself and NOT being hard on yourself will lead to personal power, health, and internal joy.

The mind works like this: If I (the mind) dissect and figure out why I am feeling this way, or why I made this mistake, then I won't do it again. I (the mind) will not only run this process through your head a 100 times, but I will never let you forget it. Because If I (the mind) let you forget the emotion or the mistake, you will lose control over the emotion, or worse yet, you will do it again. This is pure insanity and is hell on earth.

Limiting thought #1 [Dissect and figure out why I did it, or why I am feeling this.] The mind forgets that whatever we focus on in ourselves, we get more of. Self-criticism has an extreme focus in the body; it is a very intense energy that will propagate whatever it is focusing upon. I know it is very hard to get something you don't like out of your head. For example, you know how a song you don't like seems to never leave your head?

But the truth is that **we can never get the solution by focusing on the problem,** or as I say to my clients, "You will not find the health in the cancer." That is exactly what we are trying to do by dissecting the problem or emotion. For example, saying things such as, "Why did I do that," or "Why am I feeling this way," or "I shouldn't be feeling this way." If you truly forgave the emotion or situation and made peace with it, then and only then would it truly be healed and released. We just don't think it can be that easy, to **allow** the things that are making us miserable, and **that** is what will cause them to transform.

Limiting thought #2 [Fight the feeling and/or the situation enough, and I will win!] I have a picture in my office, and I tell my clients, "Don't focus on the tree in the picture;

don't look at it." What then is the first thing the mind goes to? Well, you guessed it, the tree. So many people do not want to feel the feelings they are experiencing or be in the situation they are in.

But, the only way to take your focus off the emotion or situation is to begin to accept it. This is the ultimate paradox; the only way to **move out** of an emotion or situation is to truly be All Right with how they feel and where they are. We all want to be at the top of the staircase when we are at step one. But, we must make peace with where we are standing before we can take a step. If we constantly said, "It is All Right where I am," we would have the most powerful growth in our lives.

Remember, the mind still thinks it can find the health in the cancer. What does it do? It blames and shames you for what you are feeling and where you are in life.

Self-criticism or self-blame always will stop someone's self-growth, healing, and life changes. The "blame shame game" always will keep a person stuck in the same self-awareness, job, situation, or relationship. The "blame shame game" always will keep someone at the first step.

> Limiting thought #3 [Who I am can be changed by what I am feeling or my situation.] People fight the feeling or the situation because ultimately they think they are the "mud on the diamond." They feel that they are the emotion or the bad situation. It does feel that way when someone is in an emotion or situation, but they have to tell themselves that they still remain whole and complete. That who they are at the core, an amazing complete piece of God, can never be ruined, broken, or tarnished.

It is the "mud" that grows us into more conscious beings. The same way mud grows trees and flowers, the emotion will grow you into a more loving, wise being.

> Limiting thought #4 [If I keep tabs on the emotion or situation that is making me miserable then I have control over it.] We feel if we take our eyes off what is making us

miserable, then we will somehow lose control. We don't trust the natural flow of well-being, and if we were to accept it, life would deliver to us peace, health, and joy.

We are not realizing that there is a natural flow of well-being. Remember we get more of whatever we're focusing on. We realize that we actually are creating more of what we are keeping an eye on. Many times when I guide an audience or an individual to understanding this concept, the response is, "Don't you see how miserable I am? Don't you see how sick I am? Let me tell you about it a few more times in case you forget it."

Bless all our hearts when someone tells us to Let it Go, Give it to God, Allow It, and we feel that the depth of our problem must have not been understood. We feel, "How can I take my attention off the very thing I feel will swallow me alive if I don't fight?"

Limiting thought #5 [I am a perfectionist, and things must be perfect.] What causes people the most suffering is they forget life is a process. If you understand that we always are growing and evolving, then who we are today is different than who we were a year ago or even a month ago. Trees and plants in nature that don't grow, die. Moving into a greater identity as Love, Beauty, and Peace grows us into whom we truly are. If we are the same person we were a year ago, then we have gone backward.

If we know that we never can get it done, and we are never complete, then perfection is impossible. The moment we get ourselves "perfect," then we will have the next emotion or understanding to work on. If someone tells you they are a perfectionist, they are telling you they live in a self-created hell, and they are never happy with themselves. The goal is to be happy with where you are, enjoy the adventure of life, and expect that all of life will bring to you great good. Perfection is impossible when you realize your human self will always be imperfect and will always make mistakes. As you grow to love your human self, you will realize your true soul's identity. This is a continual process, and if we are willing to deepen our connection to who we are at our core, our identity as love will continue the rest of our lives.

Limiting thought #6   [If I love myself and lighten up on myself, I will become weak.] We would not sit in a pool of self-indulgence if we were to totally love and encourage ourselves. I say if you want to lose weight, love your fat. If you want to heal your depression, love your depression. If you want to heal your body, then love your illness.

Ok, loving your illness, I know might be too much to swallow, but the way you love all these things is to accept them. By allowing the feeling, you are loving it. By making peace with your illness and focusing on health, you are loving it. You are perfect with all your "imperfections."

You have worked very hard, and have had many life experiences to get you to where you are. Everything about you is the way it is supposed to be, and it is wonderful. This perception will paradoxically allow the biggest healing and growth in your life. Ask yourself every day: Is this "thought" loving myself? Is this "action" loving myself?

Loving yourself makes you invincible. As you bring love to that which you have deemed unlovable, you reexamine yourself as love and step out of the chaos of the "shame blame game." Your human self will always be learning. But that which you have already been created to be is waiting to be remembered.

You are an amazing tree that has a few brown leaves. The brown leaves are the emotions, mind, and body. You are bigger, more brilliant, and more capable than you realize.

The mind will try to keep you small to "protect" you. We are afraid of our light, not our darkness. We reject, blame, and criticize ourselves, thinking it somehow keeps others from doing this to us. We do to ourselves the very thing we are afraid of happening if we truly shine our light. It doesn't work.

Recognize your limiting thoughts, bless them, forgive them, and then let them go. Choose to grow, choose to see who you truly are, and choose to love yourself. You have a choice of heaven or hell with every thought.

You have the keys to your own happiness. **No one can make you feel as bad as you make yourself feel.** Take responsibility for your own happiness. Stop the "shame blame game," and you will discover the happiness within you that was waiting to be found.

5

Taking Full Responsibility for Your Own Life

Taking Full Responsibility for Your Own Life

"The world is in your body; you are not in the world."

Anything we feel is because the emotions already are within us. If we choose to own our powers, we must own our feelings. Blaming anything outside of ourselves for "making us feel" the way we do blocks our abilities to experience the Love and Joy already within. Forgiving others really is about standing in our power to change our current realities.

"If someone strikes you on the cheek, offer him the other also" (Luke 6:29). We don't offer the other cheek, so that we can play the martyr and prove our worthiness to God in our suffering; we offer the other cheek because no one person has the ability to hurt you unless you are hurting yourself. We hurt ourselves by our cruel internal talks and relentless self-judgments. People can be cruel, I don't deny this, but the greater pain is when we separate ourselves from the love within. Judgment is ego; deny love to yourself because of a negative feeling, past life event, or physical limitation, and you now have stabbed yourself in your own heart.

It is not a situation that we fear, it is how it might make us feel. It is not public speaking we fear, it is how it makes us feel. It is not the mother-in-law we dislike; it is the qualities within her that also are within us. Nothing can make us feel that which isn't already within us. Love is who we are, so loving ourselves means to love the part of ourselves we have perceived to be unlovable. Bringing love to the fear, guilt, and pain is to experience within yourself that You and God have no separation. Loving our humanness or darkness is the key to happiness.

Seeing the world as a mirror into ourselves is incredibly self-empowering but can take an entire lifetime to master. This perspective is the only way to realize our worthiness and know ourselves as Love-God, otherwise we end up trying to control conditions and other people, so that we can feel good about ourselves.

The three steps to expanding our consciousness are:

1. See the world as a reflection of you! Pick the person who irritates you the most, and make an honest list of the qualities that you dislike! Courageously admit these qualities are within you, and forgive yourself. You are love and spirit; you are not your human follies.

2. Allow your consciousness to shift as you witness these qualities with compassion and nonreaction. The reality of the love will reveal the illusion. Whatever we witness disappears; whatever we resist persists.

3. Your external reality will shift to meet your new expanded consciousness.

Many people whom I have guided have stepped into personal empowerment by simply recognizing and owning the emotions mirrored back to them. Our relationships and life, as it is right now, can offer the greatest spiritual teaching and the greatest personal transformation if we simply begin to see it as a reflection of what is within us. You don't need to travel to some distant land to find enlightenment. Your life didn't happen by coincidence; everyone in your life is there for a reason. It is up to us, with our "spiritual eyes," to find the immense significance right in front of us. If we remind ourselves that nothing is outside of ourselves, we will begin to uncover the God-Love already within.

The statement, "the world is in your body; you are not in the world," can be applied in another incredibly empowering way: If we experience the feeling of great love and support, this also is from within. This feeling is not "from" them; they don't make us feel love. They might have reminded us of the Love we Are, but that Love already is within!

When we realize Love is who we are, then we never can be abandoned or rejected! The love we felt with our lover or friend never left us because that experience is within us! Love never can be lost when we realize that everything we feel is because it is already within us, and no one has the ability to make us feel any certain way.

We all have felt abandoned by a lover, a parent, or a friend. What they did might not have been very compassionate. We are judging ourselves by thinking, "If I could have been more than the person I was, maybe they would have stayed." As children, we are born full of love, so when that love is not returned, we make an unconscious decision to try to get love in another way. We try to find love by how much we please our parents or by trying to be perfect. This outside love becomes an addiction that allows us to feel lovable when the conditions are met but ultimately leaves us feeling as if we never can do enough.

Loving our darkness is the key to knowing ourselves as love. It is only our fears, doubts, grief, anger etc. ... that block our ability to remember the truths of ourselves. We all have darkness, some from childhood, and most from birth. We are growing in our consciousness, so although we create our realities, we cannot blame ourselves for the things we unconsciously created in our past. All that is God is not perfect because it is continually growing and expanding, and has no endpoint. God has come to experience Itself through our growth. When we love ourselves as we are, by accepting our negative emotions and self-sabotage, we evolve ourselves into greater Love-God. This is the process called life!

All your loved ones are "inside" of you. The experience of joy you had with them never left you. Because we believe the love and happiness we had with them is gone, we feel it as gone. As you fall asleep tonight, ask your Spirit-God to open your awareness to the love already inside you, **as you**. In the morning, you will feel the love and happiness that you felt with your loved ones.

6

Love is Who We Are

Love is Who We Are

Using affirmations to stir up the resistance to love and self-acceptance within us is a powerful and effective healing tool. Instead of repeating the affirmation 100 times, repeat once, on the in-breath for 2-3 times, and then breathe 15-20 times feeling what comes up; Feel/Love the resistance to the affirmation. Let the emotion dance through your body, and observe it, like a cloud passing in the sky. **Remove the resistance to the affirmation, and the thing you are affirming naturally becomes your reality without mental struggle.**

In guiding hundreds of people over the years, the affirmation that "stirs up the pot" the most is "I easily receive love!" Why is this? This is because in our unconsciousness, Love has been melded with pain and hurt. If love were not perverted in this way, then we would all be fully receiving of the Love We Are and fully realized avatars. (Yes, there are many people today who have reached avatar/Buddha/Christ consciousness.)

We all are growing in our ability to receive Love-God, and we all are resistant to love. **Any negative emotion and/or any physical pain simply is resistance to the natural flow of spirit-love within us. We all fight our own light.** Accepting our own divinity is the dance of life. The infinity symbol for me represents this dance of duality, believing that human and God are separate. Back and forth we go, increasing in our own awareness and self-love, and then one day, we finally come out of the birth canal, and we realize We Are the "higher self," "the master," "the angel," and it is not something we reach up to, talk to, or channel but ultimately the Essence of Who We Are. The "birth" of our authentic selves is represented as a sun and represents our realized conscious evolution as Love-God.

Why do we resist love? A beautiful spirit I was guiding explained it so well. She said, "If every time a dog ate a piece of meat, he was kicked, then eventually the dog would stop reaching out for the meat." I thought this was an amazing analogy because we all are denying ourselves the very nourishment we desire: Love. We all believe that if we were to receive love and authentically express the Love We Are, we would be hurt, criticized, or rejected.

We all have programmed within us that love is pain. This is a result of past experiences in our lives or our past lives, when we were expressing the Love We Are, and we were rejected. **In our greatest power, we experienced the greatest pain.** Unweaving the unconscious patterns we all create around fully receiving Love is an endless source of joy for me. We can mentally say, "I receive Love" all we want, but until we feel and "taste" the unconscious patterns, it is only mental masturbation. Love-Spirit is who we are; it is not a matter of creating something or making ourselves better, self-realization is a matter of loving the fears, insecurities, and corresponding patterns that we create as a way of resisting love. **Continually witnessing and accepting our perceived darkness creates a growth in consciousness that leaps us into the next greatest version of ourselves.** This is the process of self-transformation, or self-acceptance, and is the same for everyone.

Our life's purpose is to express the Love-God we are into the world. Our desire is God's and/or universe's desire. Whatever our interest or dream also is that of the universe. One person might want to be a mathematician, another, a spiritual teacher. **Your dreams are there because they are who you are.** I know a woman who loves cleaning; she even has a tattoo of a vacuum on her arm! But, because this is her interest, or her passion, every owner of the houses she cleans is uplifted by the vibration she is expressing, and because of this, she has *more business than she can handle*!! Expressing and living our true interests shifts us into the universal Authentic Self; we become the cleaner and cleaning, the dancer and the dance, the mathematician and the math.

Expressing the Love We Are brings up the greatest fear for people. This is normal, and judgment (ego) of the emotion will only make the fear worse. Feeling is healing, and self-acceptance brings love to the very thing we perceive to be unlovable.

If you don't know what your true interest is, and it can be anything, then you may have some patterns and/or attachments to unweave. This is all right. It is a never-ending process of defining ourselves from the limited to the unlimited, and it never stops no matter our age, gender, or present level of consciousness. We are all equal, and we are all divine, and we are all growing in our consciousness of the Love, God, Spirit as Who We Are. It is the dance of remembering Who We Are and forgetting who we are that awakens us to another level of our already present, expanding magnificence.

7

Transforming from Ego to Essence

Transforming from Ego to Essence

If you are willing to grow and willing to change, miracles can occur in your life. Divine presence within you desires your greatest good, your greatest joy, and will continue to *seduce you* into allowing your greatest Self to birth forth. Your Essence is yearning for you to let go, to trust, and let in all the abundance that is waiting for you. If we change ourselves, the world around us will change.

It is very important to remember, that change or self-transformation is not about *making* yourself lovable or perfecting your spiritual qualities. You already are lovable and worthy as you are. Self-transformation is a process of remembering your complete worthiness and *loving yourself as you are*, and then change is the end result. Accept yourself as you are, and change will happen.

Ego is the belief in separation. Ego is the belief our human selves can separate from Love or God. Negative emotions are the "children" of the Ego, and are our signal that we are believing in "the lie..." The lie the Ego creates is that we are powerless, lacking, and need to earn our worthiness. Loving the "*Ego's children*" dispels the Ego and shifts us into the consciousness that we are One with the divine.

By loving the negative emotions—the pain—we cancel out the Ego. Negative emotions or fear are the "proof" that we are separate from Love-God. Loving fear, we reunite our Essences, back into ourselves. Love fear, and we no longer will feel separate from God. Fear can disguise itself as indecision, worry, being overwhelmed, or procrastination. Love the fear by stopping your attempts to cover it up, run from it, or make it better. Love fear by feeling it without adding self-judgment to it. *Accept it as fear,* feel it with acceptance, and it will no longer have power over you to affect your choices, health, or life.

We are composed of four bodies: physical, mental, emotional, and spiritual. As we increase our level of self-acceptance of these four bodies, we expand in our consciousness. Everything in your life is here to evolve and teach you about your complete lovability and about the divine intelligence working in your life. **Love fear, and the four bodies will merge with your Essence and consummate the marriage between human and God.** Everything, and I mean everything, is here for your benefit IF, #1 you choose to look at it, and #2 realize it is here to teach you something about yourself, and that it is not about "fixing" the other person.

#1 requires us to look at what we truly feel about our bodies, our lives, and our perceptions of self. We must be willing to take inventory. We can do this by journaling our thoughts, meditations, becoming aware of our internal self-talk, and/or meeting with a spiritual teacher.

#2 requires us to own what we feel, bring acceptance and love to the feeling, and then identify the limited belief we have created about ourselves from this unresolved feeling. Set the intent to love the feeling, and carry this intention into the day, into meditation, journaling, yoga, exercise, spiritual session, etc. Once the feeling is processed, the question to ask yourself is, "What belief about myself or life have I created from this unresolved feeling?" The answer will come; be patient. Accept and release the belief, and then your Essence will reveal to you the unlimited loving truth of yourself. Affirm this new reality or new belief every day.

Living life as a "spiritual master" means to know that no one can make you feel anything that isn't already inside of you. For example, Steve brought this truth into his life and instead of blaming his wife, demanding she meet his needs and verbally attacking her for his perceived vulnerabilities, he began to own his feelings of unworthiness and forgive them. After a couple weeks, he was able to see that he had believed his happiness must come through another person, his wife, and he was actually unhappy with his career and was unconsciously asking his wife to fix his mood. After this realization, Steve's consciousness of God-Love within expanded, his relationship healed, and he was able to recognize the changes he needed to make in his career.

There are four stages to the spiritual growth process or birthing of your Authentic Self. The process is not linear, and we will have pieces of ourselves in step four and some pieces of ourselves in step one. For instance, a person could be in their power in their career but feel like a victim in their romantic relationship. Our lives are a spiritual journey, and as we evolve, we are continually fusing our Essences into our human selves.

#1 We are an *egg* in the womb. Life is happening to us. We haven't yet realized there is more to life than "the womb." We are not yet willing to own our feelings and change. In this stage, life is happening to us, and we are the *victim*.

To begin to move into #2, "Conception" happens (a life-changing event, an inspirational book or person, or an illness); because of this, we become willing to change and desire greater joy in our lives. In the gestation period, we read many books, take spiritual workshops, and expand our awareness of metaphysical laws.

#2 We are the *infants*. We are beginning to understand universal laws of spirit, love, and acceptance. We realize we can change things in our lives. We are learning to "walk," to trust our intuition. We are trying to own our power, divinity, and gifts. In this stage, we are trying to happen to life, we are the *"manifestor."*

#3 We are the *child*. We are beginning to surrender to our spirit. We are beginning to express our new understandings into our relationships, career, and life. We let our gifts, our power, our divinity own us. We are letting life happen through us; we are the *channel*.

#4 We are the *youth*. We are moving from defining ourselves as a personality to a presence, and we have moved from Ego to essence. Instead of feeling our life is happening to us #1, we are happening to our life #2, or we are a channel #3, we BECOME love and life #4. We are expressing the reality of joy, love, God into all that we do. We realize we are the gift, the power, the divinity. We answer our *divine calling* and become the reality of Love within.

In the desire to co-create our Authentic Self, our Essence is as strong as the desire to procreate. In human consciousness, the procreation desire has done almost too well in populating the world; the desire to co-create our Authentic Divine Self is just as strong and will propel us forward into a new consciousness of peace. Fear is swelling up in humanity's consciousness right now to push humanity through the "birth canal" and create a world of peace. We are not meant to save the world of fear and limitation but to create a new paradigm of unity, peace, and love in our world. This starts with healing and accepting ourselves, and then confidently expressing the reality of Love into all that we think, say, do, and create.

You were not born to be inert and to suffer through life. You were born to co-create your Essence and joy into the world in only the way YOU can.

8

One Light, One Power, One Presence

One Light, One Power, One Presence

God is all and everywhere. We are this light, this love, and this holy union of God. We are created in God's image: not as hands or eyes or feet, but as an energy and essence of God. Who you truly are, your true identity is that of greatness, love spirit, and joy. Your divinity is desperate to express through you as only YOU can.

There is no darkness, only the illusion that God cannot exist in all places. God cannot be compartmentalized, contained, or owned by a specific individual or religion. God is everything and everyone. No one person has the only path to God. You are

God; you are the power of the divine. Why give the keys to your happiness to another? **No one person has greater power to connect to God than You do.** We all are the same and all equal. God has no hierarchy. Unconditional love is exactly that: unconditional. God is an unconditional presence that loves all people, all things equally. *There is not a way to earn this love.*

There is no way to fight for this love. It is already here. This love is waiting patiently for us to remember its presence. God is here in all our situations and all our troubles waiting for us to change our mind, let go of our limited beliefs, and accept this unconditionally loving energy *into* ourselves. Why wait? God is here now, and Its all knowing, ever-present force simply needs us to put thought toward It.

We must let go of our clinging to the darkness. We must let go of our grasping to our pain. Painful things happen to all people. You haven't done anything wrong, nor are you being punished. Your pain is only the absence of light. Your pain is only an absence of love. Become willing to face your pain. By your willingness, you "walk" to the place you always have been. While you face the pain, be still, be very still. Then the light of the unconditional, loving energy of God will fill the pain with light. The darkness doesn't need to be transformed, fought, and reasoned with. It NEEDS the light to fill in the space. **The darkness of fear and worry only need you to stand still with them and let God fill in the cracks.** Your painful past only needs you to stand still with the pain and let God erase its reality.

Only love is real. Only God is real. The illusions of lack and limitation are not real. Our mind has created a fairy tale that God has an opposite. This fairy tale grips us and causes us to worry about money, health, and our worthiness.

Fear and pain do not need **us** to fix them. They do not need to be reasoned with, fought against, or have some expert make them go away. The darkness (fear and pain) needs the light of God to surround it. This is done by a *willingness* to receive love and a *willingness* to bring God *to* yourself and *to* your pains. Bring light and love to your emotional, physical, or mental pains. Do not try to perfect your fears, body, or thoughts; let the light of

God redeem them. There is no switch on the wall that can make darkness fill a room, only a light switch. A candle cannot be overcome by the darkness. The darkness (fear/pain) is only the absence of light and <u>not real unto itself.</u>

A lower frequency must rise to meet a higher. Physics shows us that when a higher frequency encounters a lower, the lower *must* rise. The candle's light must rise up to darkness, and God's light will rise up to your pains.

Bringing self-love, self-forgiveness, and self-acceptance to your pain brings the higher frequency of God to the pain. Trying to rationalize *why* you have the illness, *why* the past happened the way it did, or *why* you are feeling the way you do, only is trying to find the light IN the darkness. Don't bring questions to your discomfort; this is a way of trying to find the health in the cancer or the solution IN the problem. Bring love and God to your discomforts, and they will go away. Another way of explaining this is to say, "Bring light to the ego." Ego is the belief in separation. Emotional pain and physical pain are the products of this belief in separation. But the ego is only just that: a belief. Bring God to the pain, bring light to whatever your discomfort, and then the ego has no foundation.

God is right here and right now, not just on Sundays, in a church, in a book, or in a specific place. God is in YOUR HEART, surrounding you, above you, below you, in every thought, in every occurrence, and in every moment. The great blessing is that it only takes your willingness to put God at the forefront of all your thoughts for love and joy to become your reality. Bring God; bring love to all your emotions, body pains and thoughts, and God will become your reality. Bringing God to theses parts of you means to bring love, forgiveness, acceptance, and gentleness to yourself. *God is unconditional love, and this must start with your willingness to receive it for yourself.* It is waiting for you to receive it and can happen in this moment.

Your joy, your happiness are right here, right now. Let go of what must change for you to be happy. **Be happy now, feel God now, and then your life will change.** Deep breathe daily, setting the intent to *breathe in God* on each in breath. Breathe consistently in and out without any pauses. Each breath is your personal declaration to bring God, love, and joy *into* your body, mind, and life. Fifteen minutes of conscious breathing a day with this intent for even a short week, will change your life. I know it has changed mine.

Here is another tool to refocus your mind on God that might sound weird but works wonderfully. Look in the mirror, and stare in the space between your eyes, and say the word YOU three times. Draw out the O and U for 10 seconds, so you're saying, "YOOOUUUUUUUUUU." This technique begins to redefine what is you. We are human and God, not separate, but unified as ONE. The dual nature of our "humanness" and our "Godliness" is not the truth and is the ultimate lie we tell ourselves. We are ONE with our divinity, we are One with God. As you say "YOU" in the mirror, you are telling the "I" that it **is** the presence of God. The word UNION put backwards means "NO I in U." Meaning the separate "I" we have created in our minds is not real. We are ONE with God, and the 'I' we reference in our thoughts and speech is in *union* with God. We cling to thinking of ourselves as separate from God.

When you say the statement "I surrender," *it is not that you are surrendering anything real.* You are only surrendering your *perception* that you are separate from God. **When you say, "I surrender," you are surrendering the "I," so that you may become the YOU.**

God is everywhere and in everything. Another tool you can use is to say to yourself before you go to bed at night, 2 to 3 times, **"I see myself as everyone and everything."** This affirmation will help to shift your mind from thinking of yourself as separate from God.

God knows everything about you and loves you no matter what. You cannot be separate from this love because it is the core of who you are. Thinking of yourself as unlovable is like a lion pretending to be a mouse. In this analogy, if a lion could talk and it said, "I wish I were a lion. I wish I could be a big cat. I wish I could roar," you would consider this lion to be insane. This is the same with us. Your lovability and your worthiness are already within you and cannot go away. Your unique talents and gifts are within you and are waiting for you to discover them. You are the lion, but you can pretend to be the mouse; that is OK. **Eventually your greatness and your spirit *will win.*** Your light and your divinity are the reality of who you are and *will erase* any perceived "mouse-ness."

9

What is Power, and How Do I Get It????

What is Power, and How Do I Get It????

Our happiness and blissful connections to *All That Is Wonderful* God patiently waits for us to open our hearts and receive. Easily changing our perceptions of power and a willingness to feel, is all that is needed to experience greater joy in one's life!

In guiding others into personal empowerment for many years, I have seen the great resistance to this statement: "I am divine." This is because the old egoic definition of power needs to be gently reprogrammed. This egoic power is based on brute strength, money, and respect, and is secondary to spiritual empowerment. Egoic power is based on outside validation, approval, and controlling conditions to help one feel safe.

Ego power can be taken away, destroyed, and limited. Because humanity has forgotten its already present divine power within, we argue, fight, and create wars over this limited egoic power. Ego power causes a person to oppose others of different religious views, sexual orientation, personal opinions, political views, etc.

Ego power will cause a person to be continually threatened by those whom he or she perceives can take away his or her power. *This is because ultimately, egoic power can be taken away!!!*

Ego power based on outside conditions (money, control, etc.) is like a basketball game; you constantly are fighting for the ball, running in circles, and getting bruised up. Changing your perception of power raises you above the basketball game. In this position you *become the owner of the game*, directing the players, and trading them off when they don't serve you anymore. Life is the same. Change your definition of power, and you can still have money, respect, etc. but it will flow to you in abundance. *The paradox is: Let go of needing power outside of yourself, and you will have an abundance of power flowing within you.*

To remember the power already within us, we must courageously recognize and feel the blinders to seeing the power that's already there. Fear, anger, guilt, and self-doubt are lower vibrational energies within us. Observing and feeling them with non-reaction, triggers an alchemy in which the lower qualities are transformed and redeemed into gold. Self-compassion vibrates 1,000 times higher than fear, and with one thought of self-love, fear cannot live.

Open your heart, and then you are safe. Close your heart (believing this will protect you from being hurt), and you actually will attract *more* of the pain that you are trying to protect yourself from. Opening your heart and realizing the true power within and then all action takes care of itself.

True power means to love yourself, accepting who you are, accepting your divinity, recognizing your feelings. True power is knowing that by listening to your inner voice (intuition) and feelings, you always will make the right decision, say the right thing, and be the path of your highest good.

We all try to do the action (fixing, speaking) before we have done the all-important first step. The baby cannot be born without the womb or the vegetables without the garden. *Open your heart, and you will realize that true power creates the space from which all actions spring.* Once the heart is open, use the mind to stand by your convictions, apply the new understanding, and choose to live from this higher version of yourself. Speaking and acting while grounded in an open heart, is an invincible power. Your life will feel like a fight and struggle if you are speaking and acting before you have cultivated self-love.

Love, divinity, God, self-compassion, self-love, and self-awareness are the greatest powers. The true power, or the true reality, depends on us. F.E.A.R. is just an acronym for "False Evidence Appearing Real." *The false evidence feels real or more powerful only because we have forgotten how powerful it is to love and accept ourselves as we are right now.*

A life lived from the understanding of true power is easy, fun, and stress-free. Here are some steps to take in order to step into your power:

1) Begin to ask yourself what you think true power is. Be real, journal your thoughts, witness them, and release.
2) Own, recognize, and feel the lower vibrations of emotion, and allow them to be healed.
3) Make a choice for your life to be easy, fun, and full of joy. When it becomes a struggle, take the time to meditate and self-reflect.

When life becomes a struggle, it is only because you have temporarily forgotten your power, or your divinity within. But, simply committing a few moments to remembering your true power will lead you to the awareness <u>that</u> it can easily return!!

10

Why Are We All So Lonely?

Why Are We All SoLonely?

Would you like to not feel lonely again? If you are willing to change your perspective, I easily will show you that it is a spiritual impossibility to feel alone. Alone means Al-One.

The Truth Is, "When you feel a gnawing loneliness, you really are craving God or your Self." It might be hard to understand this spiritual Truth at first, but think of it this way. Do you remember a time when you felt lonely, and you went to a social event to "feel" better? Can you recall coming out of the event feeling even more alone? If you look back, I am sure you can recall an experience like this.

What was it that you really were craving when you had that lonely, empty feeling in the pit of your stomach? What you really were craving was your Self, spirit, or God. When you have the lonely feeling, you really are desiring your connection to the divine. Don't confuse this feeling with a need to fill yourself up with a new mate, a new car, food, etc. This is what most people do. That feeling never goes away from these actions because *that is not what you are truly craving!*

Think about it, if you don't have your "Self," you have nothing. If you have your "Self," you have everything. Having your "Self" means you know that you are the only vortex to abundance, love, or joy that you need. You do not need a person to take care of you or validate your worthiness. Having yourself means you know that all your needs are met, because Who You Are already is worthy and already taken care of by this abundant universe (God).

This is so important for you to know; it is **only when you have your "Self" can you truly connect with others.** Otherwise, all your relationships become "trade agreements" for love. "I will sacrifice my needs and take care of you, so I can feel loved," or "I will let go of my inner Truth and just agree with you, so I don't feel alone."

As the artist Will.i.am from the Black Eyed Pea's said, "In the pursuit to know "Self," you will come to the conclusion that this "Self" is part of the ever expanding connect."

To have your "Self," you must first admit that you don't know yourself. In Buddhism, it is said that the term "enlightenment" could be defined as "knowing 'why' you do the things you do." If you don't know why you prefer the things you do or have the behaviors you do, then you don't know yourself. Looking within and finding out why you do what you do allows you to make conscious choices about your own life. Until then, you are following past subconscious programming from your upbringing. The process of knowing your "Self" is accepting yourself, which leads to greater JOY and abundance.

Get to know yourself by watching your thoughts, feeling your feelings, and matching all your words to your inner Truth.

Observe your thoughts through journaling and see the insanity of the mind, so that you can release it. Own ALL your feelings, and realize that no person or circumstance can "make" you feel any certain way. Finally, if you don't feel or believe what you are saying, then don't say it.

In this process of knowing yourself through Self-Acceptance, you will find a great treasure. You will find your "Self" and God within. To truly BE with another, you must first have your "Self." When you have your "Self," you do not ask energetically anything from that other person. In knowing your "Self," you can rest in the Presence of God within and then truly bask in the beauty in the Presence of another.

11

Sing Your Greatness into the World!!!

Sing Your Greatness into the World!!!

Your Greatness is your Authentic Self, and it is right here, right now, already within you, waiting to be expressed. Express your Authentic Self, and you will realize your much-needed presence on Earth. We need all people to courageously sing the unique song they were meant to sing and to follow their dreams. Remembering and then expressing your Authentic Self into ALL situations and with All people raises the consciousness of the world. The world needs you to be YOU, in only the way YOU can. Live your dreams, and express your truths.

> "Be the change you wish to see in the world"
>
> – Mahatma Gandhi

Your Authentic Self is your God-given gifts, your creative insight, joy, power, wisdom, and the love that you already are. To be able to fully become your Authentic Self, you must be able to express it into the world. In "giving away" your Authentic Self (your joy, gifts, and acts of love), you *become* that which you are giving.

There are three levels of expression 1. Mental, 2. Emotional, and 3. Creative/Spiritual.

Mental Expression is what most of the world does. This expression is based on what is right before our eyes. It is based on the facts, which are from past experience, and **has no ability to have greater insight about the future.**

Emotional Expression is based on how we feel about a situation. Emotional Expression requires a person to have an awareness of his or her own emotions and a willingness to take responsibility for them. Emotional Expression has the ability to create change and inspire hope in a person's life.

Creative/Spiritual Expression has the ability to rise above "what is" and see the solution, even when others cannot. Creative/Spiritual Expression is what can inspire another individual, a business, a country, and is the expression of great leaders. Creative/Spiritual Expression is your gift, passion, or unique God-given talents already within you. <u>This level of expression cannot awaken within a person if he or she does not have the foundation of Emotional Expression.</u>

The levels of our expression are directly related to our levels of self-awareness and self-love. Mental Expression is not risky and requires someone to know theory, facts, dogma, and data. Nothing personal is revealed, and nothing is exposed. Emotional Expression is risky and requires a person to have strength and inner courage to begin to reveal his or her inner truths. It is amazing in our society that we believe emotions are weak. *Would you listen to a leader who has no feeling or passion behind what he or she says?*

Effective Emotional Expression requires a person to take the time to know what he or she is feeling. Self-Acceptance and self-awareness are essential. Journaling is a great tool. Write down your feelings, not to analyze and critique them, but to observe, feel, and understand. Don't try to do this in your head. Getting out of the mind allows you to discover a greater truth and depth to life. Your emotions are the key to developing Creative/Spiritual Expression and essential in being able to express your gifts into the world. Give your emotions compassionate attention on a daily basis, and you will have the greatest tool to living an empowered, joyful life.

Emotional expression must start in our immediate relationships if we are to effectively use it in other facets of our lives. Healthy emotional expression requires you to own the feeling but *still to reveal it*, for your own sake. For instance, speaking to your loved one, "I am sad that you don't spend more time with me. I know I can't control your actions, but I have to speak how I feel." Owning, loving, and expressing the sadness will allow you to release it. You are responsible for loving yourself, and if you don't express your feelings, no one will do it for you. *You are speaking this to honor yourself and stand in your power.* You realize you can't change the behavior of your loved one, but you have to love yourself by speaking your feelings. Owning your emotions and speaking them without trying to control another will lead you to greater self-expression and self-confidence.

Many times, people resist speaking their feelings because they don't think it will change the other person. This is not about changing <u>them</u> but transforming *yourself* into greater happiness and empowered expression. You are saying what you are feeling to honor yourself and <u>not</u> to argue the details and get caught up in an "I'm right, and you are wrong discussion." Emotional Expression, with owning your feelings, will lead to a positive change in the relationship and open up your Creative/Spiritual Expression to another level.

Many people are trying to find their purposes and passions in life. But how can they express their gifts into the world if they haven't mastered emotional expression? *It is impossible.* A person will NOT face the risk of having his or her gift rejected if they haven't yet faced the risk of emotional rejection. The ultimate goal is expression without attachment to the reactions of another. Sing like the songbird in the morning; speak your emotions and later your Spiritual/Creative Expressions for *the simple joy of being alive.*

The purpose in life is to remember your Authentic Self and then express this greatness into your life in only the way you can. Whatever you have a great interest in, or passion in, *is* your unique talent. Your passion can be anything; accounting, mothering, cleaning, healing, beading, dog grooming, etc. Follow your passion, and you will discover a great talent within yourself. Dare to express your Authentic Self fully into your own life!

12

Your Life is an Expression of God

Your Life is an Expression of God

Your life is an expression of God. What does this mean?

We compartmentalize God. We believe God to be in the sunshine but not in the garbage. We believe that God does the "good" things in our lives but not the "bad." Nothing is separate from God. Everything and every part of your life is an expression of God.

Choosing to see God in all things, including yourself, is the choice to be either the victor or the victim in your life. You either are happening *to your life,* or your *life is happening to you.* You are the most powerful force in your life.

God is life. Life is God. This means your life is here to evolve your soul. Everything in your life is about you and *in your life for a reason.* Your life, or your world, is a mirror into yourself. Choosing to see your life as a reflection of yourself empowers you to take responsibility for your unexamined perceptions and make changes within yourself. Your relationships, work, finances, sexuality, and creative endeavors all are a reflection of what you believe about yourself. Believe you are not worthy, need to sacrifice to be loved, and your relationships, finances, and position in life all will reflect your perceptions of Self. Believe the empowering truth about yourself, and all these things in your life will change

The way to love yourself is to admit, own, feel, and ultimately accept what you do not love about yourself and your life. I know it sounds counterintuitive. But if YOU already are here, meaning your soul, your greatness, the Love-God that you are, is already here, then why isn't your life one big ball of joy? Because we all have "Mud." The Mud is our pain: fears, insecurities, grief, mental racing, and our habitual escape patterns from all this pain. Clear the Mud off the diamond, and then the diamond that is you can shine. This process is simply Self-Acceptance. As you accept the Mud, what *already is there,* your greatness, your joy, your unique gifts, can be remembered. *True healing is not about fixing your brokenness or convincing you of some mumbo jumbo, it is simply surrendering to what is already there.*

Self-Acceptance is the most powerful way to transform yourself and your life because it doesn't waste time trying to fix the Mud. For example, in Self-Acceptance, rather than trying to *mange* your fears or illness, you are taught how to love the fear or illness. Any physical or emotional pain within you, is a part of YOU crying for love. A physical or emotional pain is a sign that you are holding a limiting belief about yourself. Self-Acceptance rises above the issue and recognizes the truth of who someone already is, instead of trying to fix the symptom. Self-Acceptance goes to the core beliefs that are creating the issue in the first place.

Bringing love **to** the fear or pain causes transformation rather than keeping the person trapped in trying to fix it.

Every part of your life is an expression of you. God-Love wants every part of your life to be in alignment with God. God is Life, God is Love, and God is You. God wants you to realize God *within yourself*. What does this mean? It means living your life in the greatest joy and greatest expression of YOU. This does not mean sacrifice, pain, and suffering. Show the world what God-Love looks like, by loving yourself, remembering your unique inner talents and then expressing them into the world in only the way you can.

The process of becoming YOU is a process of letting go. Even though at the time the thing or person that you are letting go of can be a painful experience, it is actually for your greatest good. *Why wait* to realize later that the job you lost actually led you to a better job? *Why wait* to awaken to the truth that the lover who left you led you to a better relationship?! You have a choice to realize that now!! God-Life is *for you* and not against you. Awakening to the spiritual truth that things are happening for your greatest good allows you to be happy even when perceived "bad" things are happening.

God-Life is a stream of love, well-being, and happiness that is waiting for you to receive it. Letting go of a pain, person, or situation allows the next thing to come in. When one person leaves, there will be others to replace them. *When you try to hold onto something that already has left you, you are not able to see the good that is trying to come to you.* For example, your lover has left, but because you still are holding onto them and blaming yourself for his or her leaving, you miss the lover who is already in front of you. Another example is a person who might be blaming the economy and the world for his or her job loss and then consequently, they miss the opportunities that are already right in front of them.

Your life is here for you, not for your neighbor or family member. *Taking ownership over your life means that you no longer need to blame anyone or anything for the conditions of your life* and from this, you no longer need to control anyone or anything to change your life. You have the power to change your life by simply and powerfully working on yourself. Your personal world will be an exact match to what you believe about yourself.

Loving yourself and accepting yourself allows you to be in alignment with the good that already is in your life. By choosing to love yourself, you become more powerful than any condition or circumstance in your life. You already are worthy, already good, and already loved. *Accepting your inherent worthiness is fundamental in knowing that Life-God is here for your benefit.* If you choose to deny your innate goodness and gifts already within you, you will remain a victim to your own life. This is your choice.

Accepting your greatness, your unique gifts, and your already present worthiness are the only ways to be in alignment with God. God is joy, God is love, and how can you possibly know God within, if you haven't accepted what God has already given to you ... YOU!

Everything in your life is happening for your greatest good. Accepting this spiritual truth is the difference between a joyful life or a life of suffering. This doesn't mean turning lemons into lemonade; it means that *everything* in your life is in your life to show you the love that you are, but only if you choose to begin or continue the lifelong spiritual adventure of accepting and loving yourself.

How would we live our lives if Love, Peace, and God were our reality? How do we make the invisible world of Love-God visible? How do we make the internal more real than the external? There are three main spiritual truths we first must discuss to understand how to practically make God our realities.

First, we are both human and divine. Our human selves are made of mind, body, and emotion. It is only when the mind body, and emotion try to operate by themselves do they get us in trouble. Mind without Spirit-God is a racing mind. Emotion without Love-God is depression. Body without Energy-God produces illness. The human self believing it is separate from Love-God is the Ego.

The second truth is we are divine. Our Spirit or Authentic Self already is here just waiting for us to remember it. Our greatness and our natural God-given Gift never goes away and can never be destroyed. Our Divine Identity could also be called our Soul, Higher Self, Supra-Consciousness, Self, or Essence.

Third is through the process of loving and accepting our humanness do we meld the connection back between our humanness and Divine Self. The disconnect between our two halves is part of the great divine plan. As we merge back our self into our Self, we expand into a greater awareness of the Love and God that we are. We experience an "aha" or epiphany that awakens us to the Truth of Who We Are. At this moment, we are grounding more heaven into Earth and raising our consciousness. This process of Self-Acceptance changes our DNA, heals our bodies, shifts our minds and heals the world.

How do you make your Divine Self your true reality? The simple answer is that you first recognize and then accept the current limited reality that you are living. Awareness could simply be described as: "You must know there is a problem to have the solution appear." Realizing we are limiting the Truth of Who We Are is as simple as recognizing how we feel. Ask yourself, "Am I Happy?" If you reply with a resounding "Yes," then no internal work is needed right now, and God is your reality. But if you have to think about it, or you said "No," then this is a good time to reconnect your human self into your divine self.

Bring love to your human self by becoming the compassionate witness to your emotions. Whatever you accept transforms, but whatever you resist persists. Healing is feeling. Journal your feelings without edit or trying to make them pretty. Feel, witness, and observe. Begin to journal everyday for a week, and you will be amazed at the transformation you will feel. You might also discover some self-limiting thoughts and beliefs that you didn't even know you were thinking. Our unexamined perceptions run our lives and biologies, but by simply admitting them and forgiving them through journaling, you will free yourself.

The invisible world becomes more real as we clear away the layers of self-judgment and emotion. The hard part of this process is first recognizing where we are judging ourselves. The critical thoughts become so a part of who we are that many of us don't even know when we are doing it! Journaling will help with this. Another tool to use is envisioning or dreaming. Admit your true dreams or goals. Many of us are afraid to admit what we truly want because the pain of where we are today is too much. Dare to dream; it does takes great courage to admit to yourself what you truly want in life. Keeping this goal in mind but still appreciating where you are is the key. Making peace with where you are in life and appreciating your current circumstances are the greatest ways to line up with your goals. Whatever you appreciate grows and changes; what you condemn now has a strong focusing energy of condemnation on it.

An amazing tool I have used in sessions and workshops is to write your highest vision for yourself on a piece of paper. Don't hold back. Some questions you can ask yourself are: What personal qualities would you like to express more in your life? What career goals do you have for yourself? What kind of relationships would you like to have in your life?

Now place this piece of paper on the other side of the room. Give yourself some space between you and the paper. Now, with the intent to love and clear any emotions or mental excuses you are holding as to why this vision of yourself cannot be true, begin to move toward the paper. Move slowly toward the paper, feeling the emotions that come up. Notice the excuses your mind might conjure, such as, "I am too old, too young, not enough education, I made bad choices ... blah, blah, blah. Compassionately witness those thoughts, don't own them, and let them go.

We must love our crazy monkey mind, forgive our fears and insecurities, and nurture and support our body. By loving our human self, we solder back together our Divine Self to our human self, we make Love-God-Joy our reality, and we become that which has always been our true self. It is time to GET REAL and let the limited reality of scarcity, inferiority, and suffering go! Love and God can only be as Real to you as much as you are willing to look within and love you. The time is now to become your own best friend and live the life God-Universe intended for you to live.

> I am bold enough to be whole.
>
> Whole enough to be free.
>
> Free enough to be Me!
>
> I intend to Be all God intends to Be as Me!

13

Engaging Your Spiritual Warrior Within

Engaging Your Spiritual Warrior Within

Expressing your Authentic Self and living your soul's purpose requires a great inner strength and focus. *You must be a Spiritual Warrior to be able to face a world that denies the power of Love and tries to conform you into a mold of mediocrity.*

Spiritual Warriors know it is important that their inner circle of people support their Authentic Expression. I used to think living Authentically meant to be open to all people and to keep my heart as open as possible. I now, thank God, know differently. The truth is that you must always keep your heart open. But, engage the Spiritual Warrior within to protect your heart.

Engaging your Spiritual Warrior to protect your heart is dependent on your ability to know the difference between Discernment and Judgment. In the West, we are so afraid of being judgmental that we don't use our spiritual discernment. Here is an example of the difference between discernment and judgment. Discernment: This person has a lot of anger and self-loathing that they are choosing to express toward those around them. I will remain aware of this within them. But, I am choosing to focus my energy toward their Divine Identity. Judgment: They are a mean and rotten person. I don't like them.

You can recognize judgment by how you feel. If you feel uneasy or separate in your observation, then you are judging. This is a great opportunity to look within, see what is being mirrored, and heal the issue. Discernment feels peaceful and a statement of "what is."

People are like a beautiful sky with a few clouds. A sky still is beautiful even with a few clouds; likewise a person still is beautiful even with a few "clouds." Discernment is to be aware of the "clouds" but choosing to see the true beautiful "sky" underneath. Discernment will allow you to make an assessment of who will support your Authentic Expression and inner growth, and who will not. If there are too many "clouds," then this person might not be the best person to let into your inner circle.

Discernment is dependent on your inner awareness of Love. You must know within that your negative emotions, thoughts, and behaviors, are not who you truly are and are "clouds." Realizing this within allows you to be able to compassionately discern this within another. You are created in God's image and because of this, your True Identity is that of Love.

You need to surround yourself with people who will validate you and celebrate your success but who also will challenge you when you are not being authentic. It is known that when two people walk together, they eventually will match each other's strides. Likewise, you only can achieve as much inner power as those who surround you.

Just because someone is a family member doesn't mean they are supporting you. Discerning this will keep you out of patterns of seeking their approval. If you are not aware of their lack of support for you, then you will *try to give to them, what they are not giving to you.* You will find yourself in patterns of over-giving and feeling responsible for them in attempts to feel a connection to them.

Another person's ability to love you has nothing to do with you. We only can love another to the degree we have decided to love ourselves.

Because you are engaging the Spiritual Warrior, *your heart actually will open even wider.* You will be able to love a person where they are and accept them just as they are. You no longer will feel threatened by the world because you are now spiritually "on your own side." You deserve to be surrounded by people who feed your soul and nourish your greatness. Allow people into your inner circle who support your Authentic Expression, and courageously let go of people who do not.

You deserve to fully remember the truth of who you are. You are uniquely talented, gifted, and are important to global consciousness. There are more than eight billion ways that God is seeking to reveal Itself into the planet. You are an incredibly important piece of the puzzle, and the world needs every piece of the puzzle to be complete. Loving yourself is the way to love the world. Your inner personal transformation is the way to transform the world.

14

Delicious Abundance Is Waiting

Delicious Abundance Is Waiting

I had the honor of being raised doing Qi-Cong and Karate. My father is a great teacher of Karate and Qi-Cong. As a young child, I learned how to fight, stand my ground, and direct my energy (Chi) . By the time I was 11, I knew how to move energy through my body and how to move energy into my fists to fight.

The energy work I learned was from a masculine approach. Masculine does not imply a gender but rather a type of approach or perspective. Standing in your conviction, spiritual discernment, and inner focus is the divine masculine to spirituality. You did not just "allow" the energy to flow in the masculine approach, you directed it, moved it, and made it happen.

Acceptance and surrender are the divine feminine. The feminine approach to energy work and spirituality is to receive, accept, and simply let the energy flow. You do not have to direct it or make it happen. You just let it in.

Recently in the last year, I have felt a wonderful merge of the divine masculine and divine feminine within me. It was as if my "Karate side" merged with my "Spiritual Healer side." The divine masculine and feminine are equally powerful, and we need both to achieve inner balance and power. The merging of my two sides has brought me full circle, allowing me to expand exponentially in my consciousness and understand the Power of Acceptance (divine feminine) and importance of Spiritual Discernment (masculine) on another level.

Loving ourselves is the key to happiness, healing our bodies, creating a life of joy, and changing the world! But, how do we "do" this great feat? What is the "right way" to love yourself? Do you see the humor in this? Loving ourselves can be simple if we allow it.

In the masculine approach, you have to analyze all the reasons you don't love yourself. The way to "love yourself" is to become aware of how you do not love yourself and "love" it. Become aware of all the ways you self-sabotage and forgive yourself.

In the feminine approach, you let love in. The love, grace, and support already are there, already around you, and already within you. Let it in. In the feminine approach, loving yourself means to let go and allow what is already there.

Depending on where you are in your journey, you might need either the masculine or feminine approach. Both are important. As a culture, we miss the power and simplicity of the feminine by believing things need to be hard and complex to work. What is simple and powerful is from God-Love. What is complex is from the mind. Loving yourself through acceptance is simple. The universe is seducing you into happiness. God's will for you is joy, happiness, and peace. You have to let go and allow it in.

A monkey sees a room full of delicious fruit. But on the table in front of him is a jar with an apple. The monkey decides that because the fruit is in the jar and harder to get, it must be better. Gripping the apple, the monkey tries to pull its hand out of the jar. The monkey's hand is too large to fit through the jar's opening with its fist closed around the apple. Getting its hand out of jar will require the monkey to let go of the apple. Then, it can have a whole room of delicious fruit. But, the monkey continues to pull on the apple and try to push his hand through. We are all like the monkey, choosing to hold onto things (limiting beliefs, toxic relationships, old habits) denying ourselves the peace, abundance, and joy that surround us.

In the feminine approach, "hold on for dear life" becomes "let go for dear life!" Love-God-Spirit already is there waiting for you to let it in. Your Authentic Self, the complete piece of God that you are, is waiting to be remembered. You just have to let go and allow it in.

For example, the moment you release the need to figure things out, the answer that always has been in front of you will reveal itself. The moment you release the need to change something, change will happen. The moment you release the need for approval, you will have the approval that always is there. Needing approval is like needing a head! By "needing" a head, you deny the "head" that already is there! It is OK to have goals in life, but desperately needing something only causes you to make all your choices out of that need and scarcity thinking. Release the need, and what already is there will come into awareness. Use the following affirmations. Say them a few times and simply allow the need to release.

Let it be easy.

"I release the need to figure things out."

"I release the need to change."

"I release the need for approval."

Then, breathe in, and allow the approval and wisdom that always has been there to surface. Allow yourself to surrender to the infinite possibilities of Good-God that are waiting for you. Repeat the affirmations a few times. Don't repeat the affirmations 1,000 times, trying to mentally "make" them happen. Say them a few times, and then allow. Let yourself feel and embody the words you say.

"I am open to my highest good."

"I let go and allow."

"I trust life is for me."

Love-God-Your Amazing Spirit is waiting for you to let it in. It never goes away, and even if you have forgotten your greatness your whole life, it is never too late. Let go, and allow what already is within you to shine. Claim your miracle; it is waiting!

15

Accept the Love You Are!
You Are Already Worthy
and Uniquely Gifted!

Accept the Love You Are! You Are Already Worthy and Uniquely Gifted!

We fight for it.

But it cannot be lost.

We will die for it.

But it remains right in our grasp.

We will manipulate and lie for it.

But it is already within us.

We will sacrifice our fundamental needs for it.

But it is there, patiently waiting for us to remember it.

LOVE is always here, always present, always within you.

You are Love.

The YOU that is YOU is always here.

You remain worthy, gifted, and loved, even when you are anxious.

You remain powerful and a co-creator with love, even when you haven't attained a goal.

Love is always with you, surrounding you, protecting you.

I am Here.

You are Here.

Love Is.

You Are.

I Am.

My whole life has been a series of actions to prevent the "loss of love."

<u>I'm Done!</u>

The fear, all fear, is a fear of the loss of love.

Attachment to something validating me, to Feel Good – Feel God – becomes a continual loss of self or loss of love.

I need no thing outside of me to make the LOVE I AM real.

I deserve to exist because I do. I deserve to be alive because I Am.

Caring what another feels about me is the failed attempt to control the Loss of Love.

I am here for Me.

I am here for God.

Done. Accomplished. Over.

I am in an adventure in Paradise,

I am a complete expression of God. I Am here.

Love cannot be lost because I am the Love I was seeking.

I am.

The picture included with my poem is of my mother and I walking and singing on a path during a Self-Acceptance Empowerment Retreat. The white orbs are the thousands of angels that surrounded us. There are many pictures like this one from the retreat. All participants at the retreat had photos of angels surrounding them indoors and outdoors. The photos where taken by different people in different areas, with different cameras, and All with the same results. In this picture, you can see the reality of Love-God that surrounds us always. The Angels, God, and Love always are around you, and it only takes a willingness to see them, to See them.

I have the joy and blessing of having a mother as a fellow spiritual seeker. She has benefited greatly from the self-acceptance process, and at the age of almost 70, she said, "I was out on my daily walk, and I decided I wanted to run! Boy, running is kind of fun!" My mother, through the teachings of self-acceptance, has transformed her body and life. She has the joy of a child!

16

Simply Be Open and All Your Desires Will Happen

Simply Be Open and All Your Desires Will Happen

If you want all your desires or goals to appear, you have to make room for them. The universe can't put something where something else already exists. The Universe/God will never ask you to let go of something that empowers you.......NEVER.

How do you open yourself to the natural flow of good that is waiting for you? Simply be willing to grow and change your thoughts about yourself. Then, miracles can occur for you Really ... that is it!

What is simple is from Love and God. What is complex is from our mind. How many times have you seen an invention and asked yourself, "That is simple; why didn't I think of that?" Simple is genius. Simply be open to love and open to grow, and your life will get better and better.

You are the inner experience of joy, the orgasmic bliss of the divine, and the simple beauty of a baby's smile. You are your heart's deepest yearning and your voice's fullest laughter. You are the light, the joy, and inner reality of life. Wouldn't you rather identify yourself in this way? Wouldn't you rather know your true Divine nature than your mind's ramblings about who or what you "should be"? Wouldn't you rather know yourself by the identity that never can be taken away, lost, or stolen?

The process of becoming who you are is a process of letting go ... letting go of your inner limitations about yourself. Who You Truly Are always has been, always will be, and never can go away! You cannot "uncreate" yourself. Your past does not tarnish your inner light or define who you are.

You have to open the space for your dreams and goals to happen. This space must start within. This does not mean immediately taking an action, (like cleaning a room, leaving a job, or leaving a relationship). This physical action will happen naturally from your inner letting go.

Open the space within, and the desired goal might even happen without any action. This is because there is no "out there" independent of us. We do not experience reality but our thoughts about reality. We think that we are our mind, body, emotions, or stories. We are not what we "think" we are ... and thank God for that!

If an action is required, it will feel like the next logical step and will be inspired. Taking action out of an inner joy and trust allows the action to be supported by the power of the natural flow. Needing to make things happen is from a fearful need to control. Take action out of fear, and not only will the timing be off, but you might have to do the action again and again without much results. Because this action is not supported by the flow, it is difficult and feels like a struggle.

Life is like a highway of well-being and grace. What if you tried to make your own traffic laws and go in a different direction than where the flow of traffic was going? You would crash, right? But, by following the flow, you usually get to your desired destination. Life is only "against" you, when you are trying to make it happen. By surrendering to the flow of life, you will get to where you want to go, or sometimes it is even better than what you thought.

You can't "make" life happen. It is like trying to make the sun rise. You can't make your healing happen; it is the natural process that is always there for you. If you open yourself to it, your good can come. Begin to say, "YES," to life.

Surrender your will to the will of Love. Surrender your will to the will of Joy. God desires for you great joy, peace, and abundance. Surrender does not mean letting go of something that empowers you but rather that which weakens you. You are only surrendering your limited beliefs and thoughts about yourself.

Seek first the kingdom of heaven, and all else will be added unto you. Right? The kingdom of heaven is your happiness within. A vision board or affirmations align you with the good that is already waiting for you. If you knew that your good already was here or on it's way, you would be happy. Right? It is this inner happiness or inner knowingness that puts you into the flow of your good. The affirmations, goal setting, or vision boards do NOT make that good happen. These tools put you in alignment with the good that is ALREADY there.

When you are choosing to see the good in your life, you see the answers that always have been right in front of you. You realize that all your life's events are happening for your highest joy. You see the opportunity for growth in situations. Instead of seeing life's events as happening to you or against you, you trust that good is happening. Even if you don't know the "why" in the moment, you trust that it will eventually be revealed to you.

Release the need to control, to allow the control and stream of well-being that is always there for you. Release just the need to figure things out ... and then the answer will appear. Surrender the need to know "why,'" and the "why" will appear.

What if you really, really knew that there was nothing to fear? How would you live your life? What if you really, really knew that God and the Universe support your ultimate happiness? How would you feel right now? How would you act toward others if you knew all your needs would be met? Don't wait ... live your happiness now!!! Open up to all the good that is waiting for you to let it in. Your joyful life is waiting ... are you willing to let it happen? Simply be willing to be open to love, and love will happen.

17

What Is Love??????

What Is Love??????

What is Love? Why has Love become like a slippery vixen that few seem to be able to hold onto? Many don't find love because we simply are looking in the wrong place. We unknowingly look for love outside of ourselves, creating attachments to this external love. Trying to "make" Love happen by some sort of action or giving is tiresome.

Love is Who We Are and requires no action, no belief, no thought, or nothing outside of ourselves to Be. Love expressed as Who You Are is effortless.

It is important to note that we all have different understandings of Love. No one person's understanding is right, and no one person's understanding is wrong. Each person's understanding of Love is perfect for him or her in that moment of his or her life. But, **only** when he or she is *aware* of what he or she is defining as Love.

The problem is that we don't realize that we have created an attachment to love outside of ourselves. We all to some degree have limited Love to how much money we have, how much we give, controlling conditions, food, another's approval, etc. When we are not aware of our attachments to Love, we torture ourselves in an endless emotional roller coaster.

In my life, I surrender to Love and the Creator on a daily basis. Since my early 20s, I have asked that my personal will be aligned with the will of Love. This caused great inner transformations and joy. But, even with years of doing this, it wasn't until the moment I realized I had no clue what love was that I began to truly know what love is.

Admitting to ourselves that we have placed our feeling good, or feeling lovable, on a condition or object is the first step.

Secondly, making a free-will choice to change our minds, and let go of our limited definitions of Love is next. Once we are aware of our attachments to Love outside of ourselves and are willing to let go, the third step is to do nothing.

Your awareness of the attachment is all that is needed to heal. Trying to fix or figure out how to release the attachment is the mind's trick to maintaining control. Being aware of the attachment opens the "door" of the mind and heart. Once open, the Love that we Are (or Spirit) can flow in and heal the attachment. It is only when we try to analyze or try to figure out why this attachment is here do we get ourselves in trouble.

It is safe to let go of needing what we believe to be love from the condition or thing. We all do it. It is no big deal. Don't try to analyze your past or blame it on your genetics. Just let go of it. The next attachment to Love outside of you will come up. Awakening to what Love truly Is is a joyful inner expansion into greater levels of Beingness.

What if love, Just IS. The Love that we define as the opposite of hate is not love. Love is beyond the dual nature of love-hate. **What if our minds' limited definition of Love is our very source of suffering?**

Love can be expressed in giving, happiness, or a hug. But these actions do not "make" Love happen but rather are an expression of the Love that already is within us. We are delaying our feeling good in the future by our beliefs that this thing or person is needed to be happy. Remind yourself, "I do not need (Insert: condition, person, object) to be happy; I am the happiness I seek." When Love becomes the nature of Who You are, then you are free.

Can you rest as the love that you are, that requires no condition, action or "other"…..to Be? Can you simply shine the love that you are?

The following is simple exercise for realizing the Love You Are:

Write down, without much thought: "What is love?" A short answer will do. Then ask yourself, "If Love is more than that, what is Love?" Keep on asking the question and answering, until your mind runs out of answers. This simple but powerful exercise can be repeated as many times as you like. **When the mind stops trying to define what love is, it is at this moment that you begin to feel the Love that you already are.**

The paradox is, that when you begin to realize what Love is not, you awaken to the Love that Just Is. In the process of Self-Acceptance or self-realization, you continually are letting go of the world's definitions of love and rediscovering the Love that you are. You are the Love that <u>has</u> always been, <u>will</u> always be, and <u>can</u> never go away.

18

What Kind of "Bug" Are You???

What Kind of "Bug" Are You???

Each of us is like are own species of "bug." We are each unique, different, and exactly what the Creator intends.

Knowing what kind of "bug" you are actually allows you to feel more at one with others. Knowing yourself allows you to let others be themselves. Paradoxically, it is only in accepting our differences that we are then accepting of others.

Are you a "mother bug," "nature bug," "hair dresser bug," "creative bug," "healer bug," etc.? What unique blend of talents and qualities are you? This distinctive blend is your "species" of bug.

We each are a complete blessing of God. God has given fully of Itself, as You. God seeks to express Itself, as you, through you, and in you.

For fun, draw a picture of what kind of "bug" you are. Use a variety of colors. Each leg could be a piece of your unique greatness. For instance, one leg could be your ability to organize, another your gift to listen. One of the antennas could be your gift to uplift a room with your smile or give a speech. One of the wings could be your gift to see the truth in an issue. Have fun, and let your creativity flow. Your creativity is a doorway to your intuition.

You will discover the wonderfully unique "bug" that you are. We are discovering new species of insects, plants, and even animals in the rainforests. You are like your own irreplaceable species that is crucial to the balance of the whole. We know that by removing one plant, insect, or animal from the rainforest, the fragile ecosystem would be threatened, and a species may be forced into extinction.

Delivering your gifts into the planet is essential to the balance of the whole planet. There are no small gifts or a nonessential person. All gifts and people are important. This is why I chose the analogy of a "bug." By accepting your importance, you serve the planet. By accepting your gifts, you are not becoming egocentric and demanding your superiority like a tyrant. You are humbly accepting your God-given importance. By doing so, you serve to balance the whole, like a species of bug.

Without you shining your light and accepting the talented and special "bug" you are, the whole planet suffers. You are part of the "energy eco-system" of the planet. There is no one person exactly like you.

Recognize that you have something to offer. Be willing to look within and accept your God-given magnificence. Then, express All that You Are for the sake of healing the world!

19

How to Heal the World in Three Easy Steps!

How to Heal the World in Three Easy Steps!

"Om At Aka Was In" (Native American greeting, meaning "To all my relations.") Many traditions teach that when you heal, you heal for your family, friends, and even your ancestors. Your healing directly affects all those around you. The Course In Miracles says, "When you are healed, you are not healed alone."

A human energy field has the power to shape its environment. Your energy field is a transistor, transformer, and projector of the vibrations you are holding in your heart. Simply said, love yourself, and you will project love. From this projection, those around you will have to rise to meet you or leave your environment.

We let our conditions and the people around us define who we are. Taking full emotional responsibility for oneself and healing put the power back into the hands of an individual to change his or her life. How you feel shapes your environment and "vibrationally" teaches people how to treat you.

Your relationships with others reflect your relationship with God and, of course, your relationship with "self." ALL your relationships are about your relationship to yourself and God. This is why forgiveness of others always is about forgiving yourself.

Your relationship with your mother, father, friends, siblings, coworkers ... meaning everyone ... is about your relationship with yourself. Someone only can irritate you if they have a quality in them you don't like in yourself. You only can love another to the degree you love yourself. The Course In Miracles says, "In every relationship you meet, you will be crucifier or savior, determined on what you choose to be to them." This is why this perspective I am presenting takes the heart of a spiritual warrior to adapt into one's life.

Integrate into your consciousness the rest of your earthly journey that all your relations are about your relationship to yourself-God. Then you will have one of the greatest transformations into your Authentic Self. Heal yourself by using all your relationships as a mirror into yourself, and you will have authentic, lasting happiness. True happiness is knowing the Love or Divinity that You Are and feeling the ocean of support that is there for you always.

How do you do this? Here are the practical steps to healing ALL your relationships, thus healing yourself.

1. Be in a quiet place, where you won't be disturbed. Get into a relaxed state with breathing and some calm music.

2. Think of a person that brings up some negative emotion within you. Feel and breathe. Be willing to feel the discomfort. Short-term discomfort for long-term gains.

Remember healing is feeling. If you react to an emotion by asking "why" it is here or covering it up with an affirmation, food, pill, etc., it will not release. The "why" or "aha" only comes AFTER you feel it with nonreaction. Don't ask why, *just feel.* Don't cover up the emotion with affirmations or food, *just feel.*

You are not your emotions. It is just mud on the diamond. You already are innately worthy, gifted, and beautiful. The emotional pain and negative thoughts are mental creations. They are not real and not the truth of who you are.

Also remember that an emotion cannot arise in you unless it is already within you. *It was there yesterday.* This person is not *creating it within you,* just triggering it. No one has the power to take your peace unless you choose.

Layers of discomfort or emotion will arise as you think of this person. Sit with it. Let each wave come up until you feel clear. As you change the vibration where you are, this person will no longer be able to take your power. Then, they will have to rise to meet you or leave.

3. When you think of this person, and you don't feel another layer of emotion arising, use this powerful clearing declaration. God gave this declaration to me in a time in my life when I had a lot to forgive within myself. I have used this in sessions and workshops with amazing results.

Visualize this person and say, *"I forgive you. I forgive myself. As I release you. I release myself."* As always, if emotion arises with the forgiveness declaration, feel and release.

By applying and repeating steps 1-3 with all your "relations," you are healing yourself, healing others, and being the change you wish to see in your world. Wow! eh?

Why and how does this process work? By feeling the negative emotion without reaction, you *are bringing love to that emotion.* You are loving within yourself that which you have deemed unlovable. This affirms to your subconscious mind that *nothing within you is separate from Love.* This is true Self-Acceptance. Acceptance and forgiveness are your main purposes on Earth.

By knowing for yourself that nothing is separate from God-Love, then you can know that for others. By knowing others as Love and a complete part of God, you no longer will perceive them as "other" but rather an extension of yourself. It is only when we perceive people as *"other"* can we feel threatened.

By vibrating within the reality of Love that you are, you see the darkness of the world as powerless. One person using steps 1-3 in his or her world could change a whole family, business, and community. Your healing is that important.

Om At Aka Was In!

20

Stand In Your Power as Love

Stand In Your Power as Love

There is nothing to fix because you are not broken. There is nothing to heal because you already are healed. You already are everything God has created you to be ... right now. In the self-acceptance process, you are "clearing the mud off the diamond." The "mud" is the emotion, pain, or limiting belief that is not real unto itself. Remember all that you Are is already here.

The paradox is that to love yourself, you must witness and feel where you are "not" loving yourself. Sounds like fun, eh? Well, when you realize how much these little perceived unlovabilities are affecting your life, it is fun to release them.

Sure, we all do physical things to hurt ourselves (bad diet, smoke, etc.), but where we hurt ourselves the most is the mind. It is not always so obvious as to where we do not love ourselves, but if you remain alert to what you are feeling, life's events will show you.

Life is always happening for your greatest good. We have a choice to remember love or fear in every situation in our lives. Every part of life has a gift to offer, even in situations that are unpleasant. Ask God, "Help me to see this differently and to see the gift in the situation. I am willing to change my perception."

Recently, I was getting a lotus flower added to my infinity and sun tattoo. The tattoo artist asked, "What does the symbol mean?" I told him that for me, it symbolized the process of looking at our perceived unlovability (emotions, pain, limiting beliefs), and from this process, we realize that we already are the wholeness and peace that we were seeking. He replied angrily, "No! We just have to believe in Jesus, and that is it!" I replied, "I am not disputing your belief in Jesus. I am just saying that our relationship to the God/Christ can only be as strong as our relationship to ourselves." He said, "We are not meant to do anything. We can't. Only our belief in Jesus can save us!"

I replied, (now aggravated), "We have to turn our wounds up to the light of God by admitting they are there and feeling them. Then, God can heal them. It is like turning an upside down bowl full of mud, up to the cleansing water." At this point, I noticed my aggravation and realized I had become attached to my expression, so I changed the subject.

Later in meditation, I realized I was attached to him "seeing his stuff" as a way of protecting myself. I had a self-limiting belief that if he saw and dealt with his emotions, I was safer. I then released (or accepted) this belief and the fear behind it. From what some would call a small interaction, I saw myself move into greater detached expression in all areas of my life. It wasn't as if I wasn't expressing in a detached way already in my life; I just opened to another level. We always are opening to another level of who we truly are, if we are willing to look within.

Try to edit your heart, and you lose your inner guidance. Match all your words to what you truly feel and think, and you will uncover your Authentic, wonderful self. You must be like a songbird in the morning, singing your song for the sake of being alive and the joy of expressing who you truly are.

Why couldn't the tattoo artist believe in Jesus and trust the process of clearing his own self-limiting thoughts and feelings? I saw that his "rigidness" was a way to keep himself from having to look within, and it was his way of feeling safe in the world. He couldn't even consider what I was saying because he was unconsciously afraid of his emotions. I knew this because he was not telling me as a matter of fact or with passion, but with rage and an attachment as to whether I agreed with him.

Your inner truth is real without anyone "making" it real. "To thine own self be true." If you don't listen to yourself (your gut feelings), then you have lost your greatest protection in the world. The "art" of listening to yourself takes practice. Be very forgiving with yourself when you don't listen.

When you become strong enough to trust your own heart, you won't find others not agreeing with you, or "getting it," so aggravating.

I commonly have heard people on the "inner self-growth" path say, "Why can't they see their stuff!" or "The world needs to wake up," or "My family thinks this self-love and natural healing stuff is witch craft!" I agree that the world needs more love and self-accountability. But if you are anxious or aggravated with the world, it is only because **you** feel threatened. And underneath this aggravation, you are not taking the time to listen to your own inner truth. People won't listen to you until **you** listen to yourself.

Love yourself when you don't listen to your own heart. Become stronger in the power of love, authentic expression, natural healing, etc., for yourself. And as you do, people will begin to listen to you without you even trying. As you love yourself, the Truth will vibrate through you, as you, in you.

Later, after I accepted myself from the tattoo experience, I went for a massage. The massage therapist spontaneously said to me, "I love when you come in. You remind me to be true to myself and look within, just by your presence." Because I listened to myself, Life/God heard me.

When you love yourself, you naturally express the light within. All of creation will sing your song with you. **As you trust your heart and inner knowing, your song is reflected back by everyone you meet.**

In your life, continue to question your true motives or beliefs. Get clear as to why you do what you do. Clear the mud off the diamond, and shine brightly. In the detached expression of your inner truth, you sing the song of your Authentic Self and become the greatness God intended you to Be.

21

Tao of Dog

Tao of Dog

"Tao" means road, path, or way. So what is the Tao of dog? A dog's natural way is to be balanced and peaceful. We unknowingly train our dogs away from this natural balance by not providing enough exercise, discipline, and affection. This principle directly correlates with our own self-care of body (exercise), mind (discipline), and self-love (affection).

Also, not providing calm assertive energy leads a dog to be nervous, misbehave, or worse yet, be aggressive. I found this out first hand when I adopted two female pit bulls from the humane society. The first month went well; but then a busy month of work resulted in the girls not getting enough exercise and discipline. (I call the dogs "my girls.")

They got my attention by attacking each other. I had a choice to blame them, the breed, or some other external factor. But the truth was, it was me.

We have a choice to see all behavior as either a cry for love or an act of love. I chose to see this as a cry for love. My girls were amplifiers to my emotional vibration. Just a tiny bit of worry, and they would react. Just a tinge of anger, and they would NOT listen to me. (Our animals and children will amplify our emotions.)

I had to clean up my emotional vibration to a level none of my intensive spiritual training and years of self-healing have ever demanded. I had to face what Buddhist teachers such as Pema Chodron call "ubiquitous anxiety". The subtle underlying anxiety that is so easy to cover up with a cell phone call, dishes, the next thought, etc... I am so thankful to God and my girls for transforming me to yet another level of peace. I also had the assistance of a wonderful "dog whisperer."

I had to be the pack leader to my girls and practice the empowered masculine principles of conviction, will, focus, choice, action, and determination. I was so practiced in the feminine principles of surrender, intention, acceptance, and emotional allowing, that I found myself awakening to a new understanding of the empowered masculine. (Feminine (yin) and masculine (yang) do not mean gender but rather an energy or awareness within).

The masculine becomes empowered by the awakened feminine. Can we assert a boundary or need if we haven't accepted where we are? How can you speak your needs if you don't first accept that you have a need? If you assert yourself without peace, then the assertiveness will create more fear and a need for control.

Discipline or structure is a form of self-love when it comes from the intent of love. The intent shapes the action. **Action without love is just violence.** For example, "Do I eat this salad because I love my body or because I feel I am ugly and have a fat butt?" The intention behind eating the salad shapes whether I stick to eating the salads or I give up later in the month from self-frustration.

The empowered masculine provides the rules or discipline for expansion. Once the person has expanded beyond those rules, the rules are meant to change.

For example, as a dancer is learning her trade, she has raw talent. She learns the rules or techniques to harness her gift. But once she improves and reaches a level of self-mastery, the rules will either change or leave altogether.

Realizing your inner gifts, power, and greatness is no different. Have the conviction to follow your truth, live from your highest intent possible, and apply your authenticity into your life.

In the unempowered masculine, rules, dogma, structure, and keeping things the same are the main intent. Success is measured NOT by how happy or empowered an individual is, but rather by how well they have followed the rules.

In the empowered masculine, you focus on love, choose peace, and stick to your convictions but still while noticing how you feel. For instance, affirm the positive and your inner truth as long it feels good. But if you are feeling bad, then allow that emotion to be felt. What you feel with compassion is released. (Feeling is healing.)

Too often people will try to simply "think positive," without practicing emotional awareness (awakened feminine). What we judge, we get more of, or what we resist persists. How can we have a vision or a goal if we are too busy resisting and fighting "what is"? Accept "what is," and then envision your good.

Practicing the empowered masculine means to make a promise to yourself and keep it. When you keep your word to yourself, you can trust yourself. When you don't provide any structure or rules for your life, you will feel your life is out of control. It is only when we feel out of control inside will we try to control external events.

Schedule your self-care: meditation, playtime, journaling, good food, water, and rest. Set your goals for the day, and then allow the day to un-fold, and trust everything is happening for your greatest good. This is the balance of masculine (goal) and feminine (allowing).

Traditional business is an example of unempowered masculine: Focusing on just the goal and profit without any concern for the well-being of the individual.

Discipline is the "father" energy that helps us to feel grounded, calm, and safe in the world. If you don't stick to what you truly feel inside, and apply this in your actions and words, how can you trust yourself? How can you trust life? You can't.

But, by the simple act of planning to exercise 20 minutes 3 times week and sticking to it, you can grow your trust of yourself and life. The small things powerfully affect the bigger picture. For example, you could affirm a positive statement in the mirror every time you use the restroom and begin to change your life!

You don't have to be perfect, if you "mess up," practice the awakened feminine by forgiving yourself.

At different points in your self-growth, there will be times that "enough is enough." You become sick and tired of being sick and tired. You are stuck in analysis paralysis, and you feel you are rehashing the old. This is the time to apply the empowered masculine, and assert and affirm your goodness. This is the time to "just do it," and move into action and get the energy moving. This is the time when if someone was to say, "You know what you need to do," you would know exactly what they were talking about.

In general, the world has waaaayyyy too much unempowered masculine and not enough feminine. But it remains important to remember one is not better than another; we need the balance. When you are balanced in your feminine and masculine principles, the peace that is within you, will surface.

Peace is not passive. As I was able to maintain peace in all times of my day, my girls came into perfect balance. As you make inner peace your No. 1 goal in life, your physical world will change.

Our animals and children need peaceful discipline to allow them to feel safe and protected in the world. We personally need self-discipline to be happy and peaceful.

Me and My Girls

22

Living in Integrity with Self

Living in Integrity with Self

When your heart is open, you feel a connection to others, and you are able to truly receive and express love. Living in integrity with yourself means you let your external match your internal. Your heart and thus your joy will open to the degree that you honor your inner truth.

Keeping your heart open doesn't always feel good. Sometimes it really hurts. Make the choice to keep your heart open for your own sake, for Love's sake, and to allow Love to live through you ... as you.

Having the spiritual wisdom to know that an open heart doesn't mean that you always will feel good is the difference between innocence and naïveté. Joy is your reality to the degree that you embrace the pain. But what you love or embrace is released.

"My girls" taught me the final lesson. After two months of training an hour-and-half per day, I had to accept "what is:" They were going to fight when I wasn't around; they needed a single-dog home.

It felt like I was being given a choice to cut off my right or left hand. It would have been easier for me to just close my heart and give them both away. But I am the one who has to be alone with myself and look me, in the mirror.

I made the choice with the intention to Love and from what felt right in my heart. I gave away the one who was most adoptable.

Your intention shapes your actions. Intend to act from love but also be authentic to what you truly feel in your actions and words. Learning to trust that your heart's expression will bring more joy in your life, takes practice.

Matching all your words and actions to your heart's truth keeps you in integrity with yourself. How can your heart be open, if you don't take time to listen to it or take action from it?

I got to thinking, "What if we all followed our hearts without needing to prove we are right?" What if you decided that the most important relationship in your life was your Self and God? **You could have an ocean of people approving of you, but it is your own approval that you are seeking.**

Without realizing it, we base our choices on what others will think. Or, we might survey our friends, coworkers, or check the facts to make our choices.

Ask yourself this: "If I knew fully that I already am loved. If I knew that I couldn't DO anything to destroy or earn the love I already Am. What choices would I make in my life?"

Following your heart's truth does NOT mean imposing your truth on another. Your truth is your truth only. Everyone has his or her own heart's truth to follow. If someone doesn't see something the way you do, don't feel threatened. How many fights and wars are started because we feel our 'hearts' truths are threatened by another? This is insanity.

Everyone has his or her own definition of love. We all are growing in our awareness of what love is by discovering within what love is not. Loving yourself means to love that which you have deemed unlovable within. By doing so, you realize the love you always have been. The Love that you already are, that can never go away, is not "born" and does not "die." Love is not outside of you, cannot be made to happen, does not require you to sacrifice your Truth, and does not take work. Being the Love you are is effortless. The process to this awareness is through self acceptance. By bringing Love to that which you perceive to be unlovable and letting go of all the ways you try to "get" love through seeking approval, and giving "love" to just get "love" back.

Your heart's truth only will be as Real as it is Real to you. And that is all that matters. Take a break in the day, and ask yourself, "What do I truly feel about this?"

Your heart's truth, inner feeling or inner knowing is your own navigational system in life. Authentic expression is a great way to love yourself. Learn to trust that as you love yourself, it will bring greater love in your life.

How you see the world is how you are seeing yourself. Right? If you don't trust people, it is because you don't trust yourself. When you become so in tune with your own heart's truth, you no longer will feel the need to trust or not trust people. Meaning, you no longer have the feeling of mistrust because you have a solid trust in your Self.

As you cultivate your integrity with your own heart, you begin to hear the whisperings of your heart's passions and creativity. Listening and acting from your heart's truth in all your day-to-day interactions will empower you to bring your genius to the surface. How could you let your life purpose be expressed if you are too afraid to express your basic heart's truth?

Listen to your heart, for you will discover the inner beauty of who you truly are, and then you will have a life that reflects that beauty.

23

You Have a Choice

You Have a Choice

We always have a choice. Fear would have us believe that we are in a hopeless situation.

But do **you** live in the paradigm that life is out to get you, it is survival of the fittest, and you must "get yours" before all the good is gone? Or do you live in the paradigm that Life is **for** you? That your Life is a spiritual experience that flows in rivers of possibilities, infinite good, and love, and that all you need to do is let go, choose love, and take inspired actions from love to have the infinite good of life on your side?

Everything that happens to you is the best possible thing that can happen to you. Choose the latter instead of being the victim of your own life, and you shall be victorious. Let go to your good, from the get go, and you will activate the harmonizing principle of life.

When our minds are ruled by fear, we take actions that only are a reaction and expression of fear. When fear has its grip on a person, he or she truly believes they do not have a choice. A person's actions to the outsider may look illogical or cruel, but to a person ruled by fear, his or her actions make perfect sense. In the moment, the person truly saw no other way.

Don't describe what you see. Describe what you want to see. What you seek, you will find. Ask to see things differently, and be open to make changes in your thoughts and beliefs. What you perceive will be your reality. Be willing to change your perceptions and be courageous enough to envision the life you want to live. Eventually, your life will line up with your inner perceptions of Love, Abundance, and Beauty.

There is a spiritual solution to every problem. Your life is supported by the divine intelligence of creation. Your heart is held by the hands of the creator as the most precious gem. Your incarnation is important, and your life is here to support you, if you allow it. Trust your life.

You are a spiritual being having a physical experience. You have been assigned to reveal the harmonizing good, prosperity, creativity, and greatness that is you. You are meant to bring heaven to Earth.

Bring love to fear. Don't make yourself wrong for being human. We all have fear; it's OK. Be aware of it, and forgive it. Forgive fear, forgive yourself, and only then you will be capable to NOT let fear rule your mind and actions. That which we resist gets bigger, that which we love, transforms. Eventually, the fear will leave through love and observation. The fear will not leave through self-judgment, suppression, or continuous action.

Be still and let yourself feel it. Then as you do, be willing to see your situation differently. Your perception is your lenses to what you see. Once you are willing, let go. Invite the new perception in; don't try to force it, go looking for it, or try to make it happen. Say to yourself, "I am willing to see this differently," and then distract yourself; go for a walk, clean the house, call a friend, etc.

Observe and bring love to fear, and a willingness to change your mind are important components to living an empowered, joy-filled existence. The third piece of advice I can offer to you is ENGAGE your life. You must show up to your own life to have life work for you.

Your life is for you, flowing, ebbing, and there right now waiting for you. Are you taking actions on the things you can but letting go of the things you can't? As a population, we want to give away our power to an outside authority. Do you listen to your inner truth and act from it? Or, are you continually looking to others to know what your truth is?

Are you communicating your wants, feelings, and inner truths in a detached way in all your relationships? You only can trust life to the degree you trust yourself. Detach from how others respond; don't seek their approval or fight. Be true to yourself by voicing your feelings and truths, and let the other person own their journey.

A wise person allows people to help him or her. Remember that this help should not come at the price of shutting off your own inner voice or inner knowing.

Your life, if you let go from the get go, will lead you to your greatest good. There are no problems in the mind of God, only opportunity. Life will not wait for you. Engage the day, let go of the details, and envision what you want your day and life to look like. Then know it to be so. Let the how, when, and where to your vision be handled by creation.

As I was listening to the radio while eating some yummy Thai food one night, I heard a song by Ozzy that said, "Life will not wait for you my friend." In my perception, this song was telling the listener that if he or she engaged life, life will carry him or her to the next greatest good and the next greatest version of themselves. Not sure this is what Ozzy meant, but my perception saw the gem to reap from the song.

All of life, the songs, struggles, and even what you might consider the boring, has opportunities for joy, wisdom, and good. Choose to see the opportunities in all areas of your life. It is there if you are willing to look for it.

You are a distribution point of creativity, harmonizing good, and joy. You are a full expression of the divine, and if you invest in yourself, you will see great miracles in your life. You are bigger and more capable than you think.

24

Let Your Voice Be Heard!!!!!!

Let Your Voice Be Heard!!!!!!

The world has its hand on a hot burner.....smiling. Why do so many people suffer in silence? Why don't people know that happiness is their divine birthright?

Is it because we are afraid to change? Or is the issue even deeper? A person **might not even know** that they deserve better treatment or to live better. They may not even know that happiness is even possible, and a choice they have available.

How often does someone say they are "OK" when they really are not? How many times have you said, that you have accepted something, but really, you are just tolerating the issue, hurting inside, too embarrassed to ask for help? Acceptance does not mean sacrifice, or putting yourself in harms way.

Acceptance or surrender feels; exhilarating, freeing and joyous. Giving up, or denial, feels; dull, boring, lifeless, and numbing. Acceptance is knowing the immense power you have to change your life, by choosing to love yourself, and being true to your own heart in all the words you speak.

The people of the world are too quiet. We can feel in our bosoms something is not right. A person can feel in their soul when innocence is being tortured. But we remain silent. And if we do take a stand, we will soon take back our words. We will dismiss our feelings as being too sensitive, unloving, or too emotional.

People of the world wake up! *Your sensitivity is the consciousness of your family and the planet.* Before every great change there needs to be a revolution. If nothing changes, nothing will change. If you don't take a stand for yourself and what you feel is right, then things will remain the same.

Remember the person that brings out the problem will initially be told *she or he is the problem.* Stay strong in your truth; listen to your heart and don't settle for less than what you know to be true.

Do you know that your thoughts and feelings are important? Have you placed someone else's inner guidance as your own? Have you become a like a chameleon? Just believing, thinking and eating to match those around you? Or do you listen to your own inner guidance, gut feelings or heart? Have you forgotten that you are your own best healer, friend and lover? Have you lost your—Self?

There are three levels of expression: Speaking from logic, memory, or the mind; Speaking from emotions; or speaking your inner wisdom, gifts, and passions. Your ability to express your wisdom and innate gifts rests on the foundation of your detached emotional expression.

In honoring your own emotions you are loving yourself, receiving love, and anchoring within your subconscious that you are important. You could have a great job, or be respected by many. But if you don't honor your own emotions, you won't be able to feel all the good in your life. **You will be starving at your own banquet, wondering why you are unhappy when you have all these good things in your life.**

First step is to own your emotions and embrace the mirror. Feel the emotion, bring love to it, and from that, it releases. Take full responsibility for your emotion do not blame it on another, condition or situation. But, once you have done this, you still need to voice your hurt, especially in a relationship. Do not voice your hurt to convince them your hurt is important. Feeling your hurt, taking responsibility for what is being mirrored and you will already know this for yourself. You voice the hurt to honor yourself, God and the relationship.

Don't speak your hurt if you are attached to them 'getting it', convincing them or proving you are right. This means you have some more processing of the pain to do. Express your hurt and remain detached from how they respond. By practicing detached emotional expression you will feel grounded in love and feel your own importance, because you have taken the time to honor your emotions.

Your voice, and your words are important. Speak your emotions to your loved one, and to your children. When you are being disrespected, own your hurt, but then respect yourself by speaking your hurt in a detached way.

Remember you are doing this for your Self, and not to convince them you are right. It is not about being right or wrong, but more about being true to your Self.

Your emotions are the key to knowing your own needs. Giving yourself what you need and/or asking for what you need is self respect in action. **You can't know what you need if you don't honor your own emotions.** If you feel people are taking from you, disrespecting you, it is only because *you are doing this to yourself.* By not honoring your emotions and giving yourself what you need you have vibrationally put up a sign that says, "Come piliage and take from my banquet."

You are responsible for knowing and giving yourself what you need. If you speak your need to a friend or loved one, do it in a detached way. For instance you may say "I need some time right now to work-out, let's do dinner together tomorrow." The loved one is not responsible for giving you what you need. You are. You must know your need is important, even if they don't honor it as so. You speak your need for Love, Self, God and to create healthy relationships.

Knowing your emotions and needs are important to having healthy boundaries. If something doesn't feel safe or right to you, listen to yourself. You are responsible for speaking your needs and boundaries. Don't try to fight or convince another. Be calm and assertive. Know it is important for you and that is all that matters. This takes great self love, confidence and self respect. You are responsible for teaching others how to treat you. Speak your emotions, needs, and boundaries in a detached way. **Otherwise you will attract people who want to challenge your boundaries and fight with you.**

Once your inner conviction, self-love or self respect becomes firm within, you may actually no longer even need to speak your needs, or boundaries because the person who is disrespecting you will either change or move away. As you change, your world will change. How you treat yourself is how you will be treated by others. Choose to love yourself.

Your voice, your conviction to love yourself and act from love, is *your* greatest protector. Your voice and how you choose to use it can be your best friend or your enemy. Silence can kill. There is no such thing as neutral, because Love is not passive. **Loving yourself, is powerful, and an open heart is invincible.** Take a stand for your Self, for Love, and for God. Speak what you need to say, but be detached from the outcome.

Detached emotional expression is the foundation in expressing your wisdom, gifts or inner truths. Honoring your emotions is like the tiny pebble thrown into a pond. As you take time to be gentle with your fear, anxiety, anger, etc... you create a ripple of Love and support for all other areas in your life. Being emotionally gentle with yourself makes you powerful, not weak. It is the opposite of what you think.

People that 'vomit' their anger on another or sound 'whiney' are **actually asking** for their hurt to be validated. They don't realize that if they took time to feel the hurt or emotional pain they would feel free. The freedom they seek is from their own self denial.

As you honor your hurt or emotional pain you become more grounded in Love. You are showing yourself that you are important and loving yourself. As you do this you feel confident enough to speak your wisdom, and ideas to others. By first processing and then speaking your emotions you are taking a stand for Love, Self, and God. By doing this you create a solid foundation for your innate gifts and talents to express in your life.

If people are not listening to your great ideas or talents, it is because you have not taken time to honor your emotions, needs, and/or boundaries. This is why loving your emotions is the core to creating abundance, support, and the life you want.

When you love yourself by practically feeling that which we deem unlovable (fear, anger, grief) you show your human self (mind, body) that it is lovable. You show yourself that you remain lovable even when you feel you are not. You show yourself that no-thing is separate from Love by simply processing your emotions and speaking them in a detached way. This is the power of self acceptance.

Speak to empower yourself, and not to prove anything to anyone. Speak to hold your ground and fill your space with heaven, love and beauty. Your voice is the way to create heaven or hell in your own life.

You stand for Love, or you don't. This is not about being anti-war, anti-hate or opposing anyone. Whatever we focus on, we create more of the same. This is about using the voice God has given you, to create peace in your life, your work, and the world. Your voice is important. Take a stand for what you feel is right, not to convince or prove, but to **be in integrity** with your own heart.

If you don't take time to feel your emotions daily and know what you truly feel, you won't be able to trust yourself, and thus you won't trust people or the world. And to the degree you trust yourself...to be true to yourself, you can feel safe in the world.

When you trust yourself you are not so threatened by others who hold darkness or pain inside. You have loved your own darkness, so you don't see it as who they truly are.

You can see their pain, but because you choose to love it, you are not vibrationally engaging it. This is not about "only seeing the good in someone." Loving someone is seeing their darkness and light, but knowing, from within your own consciousness, that the light is Who They Truly Are. You get what you focus on. Love ALL of you, and you can love ALL of others.

Focusing on love in others, you will get love. Focus on others darkness, you get their darkness. But having this love focus is achieved entirely from the internal process of self acceptance.

If you put your best friend or child in your shoes right now, would you be so complacent? Would you want him or her to endure what you are enduring? You **deserve** to be loved and respected, but you must do this for yourself first.

Lead with self-love in your words, even if it upsets someone else. Love will bring love. If you lead with self-sacrifice and trying to "keep the peace," sacrifice will bring sacrifice. Where God guides, God will provide. Where fear guides, fear will bring more suffering.

The mind will try to convince you that you are to blame for the issue. After all, isn't the more "spiritual" person the one who "has it all together?" Doesn't the spiritual follower believe she created this issue, so she is to blame for it? Or a religious man may believe, by admitting his hurt, fear or pain, he would be showing a lack of faith? Both beliefs are age-old tricks by the mind to keep a person locked in guilt. **As long as a person blames and guilts themselves for the issue, they can never be free of it.**

Life has challenges; it's not that you haven't had enough faith or are lacking in your co-creative abilities. Life is messy.

Buddhism teaches "Life is pain." **Life has pain, but how we choose to interpret it, decides whether it is pain or suffering.** Feeling pain or emotion without self judgment or reaction and you will have happiness. Run from the pain, or try to cover it up, and you will have suffering.

It is *only* when you are loving the pain, can you see the blessing in the problem and the wisdom to be gained from it.

You are love and already loved. No fear, issue, or pain can "make" you unlovable or "make" you "bad." You are, and have always been, my dearest...innately worthy. There is no losing your goodness; there is no earning it. **You are already a good person.** We all just have a choice to choose self love, or sacrifice. We all have a choice to be happy, or continue to live in denial.

Acceptance does not mean tolerance. Admit you are in pain, feel it, and deal with it. Love the pain or emotion and you will know happiness. Resist the pain and you will suffer and pretend to be happy. Acceptance of your pain or emotion brings you into the awareness that no-thing...even pain....even you, is NOT separate from Love/God.

Speak up for yourself. There is no "small" act of love. Love is never wasted. Even if you don't think it did anything, it did.

Your silence is killing you a little bit every day. You are worth speaking up for. Even though the changes and actions must come from within you, you don't have to do it all alone. Ask for help if you need it. Ask a friend to help you sort things out, go to a therapist, priest, healer, or read a healing book. It is a wise person that allows people to support them and knows how to give themselves what they need.

You don't have to endure what you are enduring. Your mind will tell you it is no big deal. It is important. Your happiness is important. Take your hand off the burner, and begin to make changes. It won't be all at once, just a little bit at a time.

Begin to match ALL your words to what you truly feel and believe. Be silent if you cannot speak in a detached non-combative way. Take time to get to know yourself on a daily basis. Simply notice your thoughts, beliefs and feelings and you will be "reading" the greatest book on the planet.

You are interesting, unique, and deserve to be happy. The world needs you to love yourself and know that you are important. Use your voice to love yourself through expressing your emotions, needs, and boundaries in a detached way. Be true to who you truly are. Happiness is your birthright and loving yourself is the way.

25

You are Beautiful Now

You are Beautiful Now

You are beautiful now. Not after you lose weight, get that promotion, or fix all your personality flaws. Your perceived flaws are beautiful now. It only is in believing you are not beautiful do you make yourself so. Everyone is beautiful and handsome, if and only if, they choose to believe so.

Working with "Jane," who at one point was a model and now a homemaker, she realized that although she and her husband of 10 years loved each other, part of their relationship was based on her looks. She realized she was a trophy wife to some degree.

Because she unknowingly had some shame from this pattern of being a trophy wife, she had sabotaged her good looks by gaining weight, cutting her hair short, and wearing drab clothes.

Our "human-self," meaning the mind, body, and emotions, will do things when trying to cope with life. Her human self had cleverly found a way to deal with the pattern of having her beauty owned, and the inner shame of living this pattern.

Jane realized consciously why she always felt like a second-class citizen to her husband – she had unconsciously chosen to use her physical beauty as a trade for security and love. In recognizing the belief and pattern, she then chose to forgive herself and thank the pattern for helping her all those years.

The belief and pattern were her "crutches" until she was ready to let them go. When someone recognizes their self-imposed beliefs and behaviors, love and forgiveness are the keys to letting go. Trying to analyze, fix, heal, or figure out the pattern only will keep you stuck in it longer. Consciously choose to not engage the pattern by not going into analysis paralysis. But when you see yourself in the old self-belief and pattern (because you will), then bless, forgive, and thank the pattern. (The belief and pattern also could be called an addictive behavior or our default identity.)

As Jane began to forgive the belief and pattern, and choose to own her beauty for herself and for God, she began to come alive again. Her sex drive came back, and she began to lose weight.

As we change ourselves, we will dip back into the old way of being a few times. One step back, three steps forward. Spiritual growth is not linear.

The only difference between someone who has achieved self-mastery and one who has not is self-forgiveness or self-acceptance. To the degree you accept your human self, you will know your divinity. Meaning, love yourself as you are, and you will know your magnificence, just as you are, right now.

As a person realizes that his or her human self always will be flawed and will always make mistakes they will stop trying to fix their human self, accept it, and by doing so, organically shift their awareness to their true identity of creativity, beauty, intelligence, spirit, and love.

Perfect is completely impossible when you are on a spiritual growth path because the remembrance of your divinity, beauty, or true self always is growing. This growth happens by dipping into the old self-beliefs and patterns, and forgiving them.

For instance, you believe you are not good enough. You over-do and over-give to all your friends in an attempt to earn their love. The pattern never works because you come from the belief of "I am not enough." It might feel good as you are giving. But because the true belief and pattern are never changed, you are left feeling empty.

As you choose to love that "not enough" belief and give love because you feel love, not because you are trying to "get" love, you will notice that even though you are not giving as much, the giving you are doing feels richer and fuller. You realize as you bless and forgive that "not enough" belief, you can choose to give when you truly "want to" and not when you "have to."

As you love or forgive that which you have deemed unlovable in yourself, you affirm to yourself or your "human-self" that ALL of you is Love and that no part of you is separate from Love or God.

Jane was able to take ownership over her beauty and be proud of her body. Her vitality, or sex drive, was able to shine, because it no longer was unconsciously asking a man to "make it real" or "valid." As this chapter of her journey closed, she said, "I realize that clothes do not make me look good. I make clothes look good."

Then she realized that her life doesn't make her feel good, she brings the goodness to her life. Then she realized that she doesn't get love from her husband, she brings love to the relationship. From looking at her beliefs around her body, Jane realized the eternal truth: "Do not seek happiness; be the happiness you seek," or "Be the change you wish to see."

Trying to "get love" from another is like two fish in the ocean. One fish says to the other "I'll give you all the water you want!" Love and beauty are like the ocean water; always in abundance.

Jane's story is a true story. But it is reflective of the hundreds of women's stories I have heard. Men are no different. They might not be asking for their beauty to be approved, but rather their power and intellect to be approved of, and those they also must find within themselves.

In owning our magnificence now, in being beautiful, powerful, and loving now, we bring that to our bodies, lives, relationships, and world. You own that which you already are and are created to be, and you will see miracles in your life. This is the promise of love, creation, and life. And if you choose to love yourself, life will bring great miracles and support to you.

You cannot get what you truly are seeking from life (Happiness, Peace, Love, Beauty, Power, Joy) because you must bring it to your life.

Life supports your magnificence but does not support the limiting beliefs and patterns of littleness. Shine your light, own your power, and the sidewalk will raise to meet your feet.

26

Encouragement

Encouragement

A tree by its mere existence benefits the Earth. Likewise, you remembering Who You Truly Are can do the same.

When you remember the love and preciousness you truly are, you shift all your words and actions into the energy of love. The intent or energy behind any action shapes the end result of that action; even more so then the action itself.

Your true identity is that of love, right now. Intend to Be love, and give love and then all your actions will bless those you encounter. Your eyes will bless all that they see.

A tree remains a tree even if you threw mud on it, chopped its limbs, or called it by a different name. Likewise you can't destroy that which you have already been created to be. No emotion, condition, or past can change the love and goodness that you are.

A tree's strong roots strengthen other trees and help the forests terrain. By grounding in joy, self-love, and your unique talents into yourself, you root your true identity, your authentic self into the planet, leading others through your living example. Your best is yet to come.

Give yourself permission to be strong. Give yourself permission to exceed the limitations of your parents, conditions, or friends. As you express your innate greatness and stand strong, you strengthen others. You can only help, strengthen, or love others to the degree you have done this for yourself. This is why shining your light, and knowing the love you are, is the only way you can express true unconditional love to another.

Release all the lies that you are telling yourself. You are not your stories, limitations, or past. If you take a chance on yourself, you will be pleasantly surprised.

Let go of all the limiting messages the media, your past, or co-workers are telling you. The world is hypnotized into meritocracy. Decide right now who you want to be. You have that free will choice.

Your emotions, thoughts, and body are like a horse. As you make the choice to simply love these parts of you, the Real you, comes into your remembrance. The Real you is the rider on the horse. The rider is your true identity of beauty and love. Stop thinking you are the darn horse.

Choose to remember who you are now. Do this by being willing to open up to life, love, and your true self. Simply be willing to be available to all the good that life wants to bring to you.

Show up for your own life and life will support you. Your life is important. You are very important to the healing of this planet. We need you. Take one step and Life/God will handle the details for you.

Stay open and remember the true secret. That you are divine intelligence seeking to express itself through you, in you, and as you.

Simply remember who you truly are and you will be like a tree, blessing all that you encounter. Wake with a mile each day, knowing who you truly are.

Choose to release all those limiting lies now. Stop seeing them as something to be analyzed, or solved. Choose to see all your limiting thoughts or stories...as just not so interesting. Be more interested in love.

Let go and let life love you. Let go and open to all the good that is waiting.

Affirmation

I am driven to live in joy, to realize God within self and thus be a living example for others.

The time is now. Humans are waking up. Love is the answer to every problem. I believe we all sabotage ourselves. <u>NO ONE ELSE</u> is responsible. It is only through the willingness to see the self-sabotage can true joy be found. I must be willing to see the self-sabotage with compassion, gentleness, and acceptance if I am to uncover my true amazing Self. I believe acceptance is the greatest transformational force in the universe. I believe nothing can upset me unless I give it permission to do so. I believe my mind, and heart are tools for life, and not necessarily who I am. I seek to empower these tools by clearing the layers of pain, fear, anger, anxiety, grief, and narrow mindedness. I do this, so I can utilize the tools of thought and feeling to create a world of my desire: a world of joy and peace. I believe I AM a light house of God's love. I Am this Love. I believe God/Love/Spirit is my true identity. I vow to embrace the love I Am with every thought, feeling and breath. I believe only when I have freed myself, can I free another.

I believe as I love myself and embrace the-light-I-Am: I will change the world.

Thank you, thank you, thank you.